RAW PORK

—AND—

HARDTACK

A CIVIL WAR MEMOIR FROM MANASSAS TO APPOMATTOX

Civil War Heritage Series – Volume X

Walbrook D. Swank
Colonel, USAF Ret.

Burd Street Press

This Burd Street Press publication was printed by

Beidel Printing House, Inc.
63 West Burd Street
Shippensburg, PA 17257 USA

In respect for the scholarship contained herein, the acid-free paper used in this book meets the guidelines for permanence and durability of the Committee on Production Guidelines for Book Longevity of the Council on Library Resources.

For a complete list of available publications please write

Burd Street Press, a division of
White Mane Publishing Company, Inc.
P.O. Box 152
Shippensburg, PA 17257 USA

Library of Congress Cataloging-in-Publication Data

Cave, Robert Catlett, 1843-1923.
    Raw pork and hardtack : a Civil War memoir from Manassas to
Appomattox / [edited by] Walbrook D. Swank.
        p.   cm. -- (Civil War heritage series ; v. 10)
    Includes bibliographical references and index.
    ISBN 1-57249-031-4 (alk. paper)
    1. Cave, Robert Catlett, 1843-1923. 2. Confederate States of
America. Army. Virginia Infantry Regiment, 13th. Company A.
3. Soldiers--Virginia--Orange County--Biography. 4. Virginia-
-History--Civil War, 1861-1865--Personal narratives. 5. United
States--History--Civil War, 1861-1865--Personal narratives,
Confederate. 6. Orange County (Va.)--Biography. I. Swank,
Walbrook D. (Walbrook Davis) II. Title. III. Series.
E581.5 13th.C38 1996
973.7'455--dc21   96-48774
                                                        CIP

PRINTED IN THE UNITED STATES OF AMERICA

DEDICATION

To the Memory of Three Brothers

Robert Catlett Cave, Reuben Lindsay Cave
and Lindsay Wallace Cave,
Company A, Thirteenth Virginia Infantry
Army of Northern Virginia, C.S.A.

CONTENTS

ILLUSTRATIONS

M<small>APS</small>

ABOUT THE AUTHOR

During his distinguished career in the United States Air Force the author received numerous awards for meritorious service and at one time was assigned to the Office of the Personnel Advisor to the President, The White House. Colonel Swank is a native of Harrisonburg, Virginia. His grandfather, Thomas S. Davis of Richmond, Virginia, was a member of the Tenth Virginia Cavalry and a relative of President Jefferson Davis. He has written or edited eleven previous books about the North-South conflict, including his award winning *Confederate Letters and Diaries, 1861–1865.*

He has a master's degree in American Military History and holds membership in the Bonnie Blue Society which is based on his scholarly research and published literature. He is the recipient of the United Daughters of the Confederacy's Jefferson Davis Medal for his outstanding contributions to the preservation and promotion of our Southern history and heritage.

He is a member of the Society of Civil War Historians, the Military Order of the Stars and Bars, Sons of the American Revolution, The Ohio State University Alumni Association and various historical societies.

ACKNOWLEDGMENT

I am indebted, and express my sincere appreciation, to Mrs. Frances Powell Gordon of Fredericksburg, Virginia, for this brilliant, vivid and fascinating Civil War memoir of her great uncle, Reverend Robert Catlett Cave of Orange County, Virginia.

I am grateful to the J. W. Bliley Funeral Homes, Richmond, Virginia, for the battle scenes at Manassas and the Wilderness.

P ROLOGUE

THE PATRIOT BROTHERS

Before this outstanding wartime memoir of Robert Catlett Cave is read, it is pertinent that we review several significant events in the lives of the author and his two brothers, Reuben Lindsay Cave and Lindsay Wallace Cave, who served with him in his military unit. Several interesting happenings follow.

Each of the men had been wounded; Robert Catlett, twice, once through the neck; Lindsay Wallace was struck in the head by shrapnel which destroyed an eye and was cut from the lower jaw on the opposite side of his face; and Reuben Lindsay had eight scars upon his person from three bullets going through his body. As he was being taken from the Spotsylvania battlefield General Robert E. Lee stopped the litter bearers and spoke a few words of consolation and encouragement to him.

Playing host for the night to a man who once tried to kill you is not a very attractive pastime. Reuben Lindsay Cave went through that unique experience without a qualm. Nor did he arise in the middle of the night, as most men would have been prompted to do, and invite the guest to finish the argument where it left off.

The story began during the days of the Civil War when Reuben Cave, scarcely eighteen years of age at the time, lay wounded behind

Confederate lines near Trevilians, Virginia, at his brother's farm-house. He was recuperating from wounds received at the Battlefield at Spotsylvania Courthouse. One morning, news came that a de-tachment of Federal Cavalry was approaching. Young Cave, weak from wounds, sprang from bed and saddled one of his brother's horses.

As he and his mount plunged out of the gate and headed to the South where General Wade Hampton's forces were known to be encamped, the Yankees came in sight from the opposite direction, one of them riding a white horse. Rifle shots rang out, and bullets whizzed by young Cave and buried themselves in the road around him. Fortunately, all shots missed their mark; but the perilous chase continued for several hours with Cave's mount only a few leaps ahead of the rider on the white horse. A scouting of Hampton's camp was encountered miles down the road, and after a skirmish which lasted all the way to Hampton's lines, Cave was delivered from the pursuers.

Some years later, Reverend Cave, a veteran and noted minister of Nashville, Tennessee, and a leader in the Christian Church, of-fered to house a number of delegates to a Baptist convention in Nashville within his own home. One evening as the guests were gathered at supper, the talk turned to the Civil War which had ended only a few decades before. Young Cave had been wounded at the Battle of Spotsylvania Courthouse and as this was discussed, a man named Wilkerson, from Chicago, announced that he had served there with the Federals. Reverend Cave's narrow escape was re-counted, and Wilkerson surprised the group by announcing after a few questions, "Why, sir, I was the man on the white horse." The war being over, Reverend Cave and the visiting minister did what many other boys of the blue and the gray have done since then, they shook hands across the table, and forgetting the bitterness of the conflict, did honor to a common flag.

In one battle along the Rappahannock River, it became neces-sary to burn a pontoon bridge which the Confederates had con-structed, and the other end of which had been captured by Union troops. In the face of almost certain death Cave volunteered to burn the bridge, and actually accomplished the feat, to the great satis-faction of his commanding general. He was given thirty days leave as a reward.

Following the war all of the brothers became prominent clergy-men.

Lindsay Wallace Cave

Robert Catlett Cave

Reuben Lindsay Cave

Cave Family Photos

I NTRODUCTION

These pages contain the brilliant, vivid and fascinating memoir of Robert Catlett Cave of Orange County, Virginia. War broke out when he was eighteen years of age and he enlisted, along with his two brothers, in the Montpelier Guard, Company A, Thirteenth Virginia Infantry Regiment. This noted military unit was one of the most frequently engaged regiments in the Confederate Army of Northern Virginia. It participated in more than seventy various types of engagements during its career— from First Manassas to Appomattox. During the conflict three of its commanders were promoted to the rank of general. Two of these were killed in battle, namely, Lieutenant General Ambrose P. Hill and Brigadier General James B. Terrill who succeeded Brigadier General James A. Walker.

Private Robert Catlett Cave, who was a member of General "Stonewall" Jackson's "foot cavalry," takes you through four years of battles and engagements with eyewitness accounts of fierce and bloody combat. He was wounded twice and his narrative brings the "Rebel Yell" to life. During the Shenandoah Valley Campaign of 1862 General Jackson marched his army of sixteen thousand men more than six hundred miles in thirty-five days. They fought five major battles and four separate Union armies, totaling sixty-three thousand troops, and all were defeated.

An inspection of the paroles granted at Appomattox Court House shows that fewer than seventy members of the regiment were still in the unit when it finally surrendered. Only twenty-two members of Company A were present to lay down their arms.

The memoir has been enhanced by the addition of maps and illustrations.

NOTHING CAN SURPASS THE WORDS OF THE MAN WHO WAS THERE

C HAPTER I

Pursuing General Nathaniel Banks

If one will draw an arrow with a triangular and broad-shouldered head pointing to the north, and think of its point as Winchester, the tip of its right shoulder as Front Royal, the tip of its left shoulder as Strasburg, and its shaft as the Massanutten Mountain, he will have a tolerably fair idea of the relative positions of the places that stand out most prominently in any account of the movement against General Banks. The Massanutten Mountain, rising abruptly between Harrisonburg and the Blue Ridge, extending northward in an almost unbroken sky-line for nearly fifty miles, and crossed by only one highway, separates the Luray Valley from the Shenandoah Valley. Just a little to the west of its northern terminus, where the north branch of the Shenandoah River sweeps around its base to meet the south branch that comes down the Luray Valley, is the little town of Strasburg; and about a dozen miles east of Strasburg, near the confluence of the two streams, is the town of Front Royal. Winchester, farther north, is about eighteen miles from each of these two towns, and would be at the apex of a triangle formed by a line drawn through all three. The turnpikes leading from the other two towns to Winchester, and forming the sides of the triangle, are connected by crossroads. This outline of the lay of the land may help to a better understanding of how General Banks was driven from the Valley.

That General had fallen back to Strasburg, and was fortifying his position there. To guard the northern end of the Luray Valley

1

and protect his left flank against any movement from that direction, he had posted a considerable force at Front Royal. General Jackson, returning from McDowell, where he had defeated Milroy, and taking in the situation, determined to move against the enemy at once. His plan, as we learned when it developed in action, was to threaten Strasburg with a small force going down the Shenandoah Valley, while his main body would move down the Luray Valley, capture or disperse the Federal detachment at Front Royal, and, by rapidly pressing forward towards the town of Winchester and along the crossroads leading to the turnpike between that place and Strasburg, get completely in the enemy's rear. It was an admirable plan, but it required the utmost secrecy and almost superhuman expedition to make it entirely successful.

Our division, under General Ewell, being fresh and already in the Luray Valley, was ordered to move in advance. On the evening of May 20th, I think it was, we were told to prepare three days' rations and be ready to march next morning, without knapsacks, blankets, or any encumbrance not absolutely necessary. Just as the sun was glinting through the tree-tops on the summit of the Blue Ridge, we left the most pleasant of all the camps in which I sojourned during the war, and marched south to the turnpike leading from Luray to New Market. Next morning, we followed that highway across the south branch of the Shenandoah River and along its zigzagging incline up the steep side of the Massanutten Mountain. We thought, of course, that we were going to New Market, but, when the head of the column reached the top of the mountain, we were ordered to face about and march back.

A young and self-conceited lieutenant who had been given a commission because he had spent a few months at a military school and could teach a squad how to present arms, being somewhat heated by the long climb, was outspoken in his condemnation of such "shilly-shallying." He said:

"General Jackson don't know his own mind. No wonder the boys at the Institute called him 'Fool Tom Jackson'. It's utterly foolish to march men about in this aimless sort of way."

"Perhaps," quietly replied the private whom he addressed, "if we knew as much as General Jackson does, we would think it wise instead of foolish." We could all see its wisdom, when we understood that it was a move to fool the Federals—to convince any Federal lookout that Ewell's division was on the way to New Market, and make him hasten to General Banks with the report that the Confederate forces were concentrating in the Shenandoah Valley for an attack on Strasburg.

Having marched up the hill to deceive, we marched down again to go about our real business. Then we got back into the valley, we took the road to Front Royal, more than twenty miles away, and bivouacked that night within easy reach of the town.

The men were told to start no fires, and to make as little noise as possible. After eating a due portion of their rations and lighting their pipes, they sat around in groups, discussing the situation. They had heard that the Federals were at Strasburg and Front Royal; they knew that we were stealthily approaching the latter place; and, putting two and two together, they got a pretty good idea of General Jackson's purpose. They had not then come to have implicit confidence in him and his plans, and some of them had such faith in their own strategic ability that they felt competent to improve upon anybody's plans. One of these—a man who had visited that section and hunted over the ground—said: "If I were in command, I'd send three or four brigades of infantry to pick their way around the foot of Massanutten Mountain and get in between Front Royal and Strasburg. Naturally the Yankees think it impossible for us to get at them from the mountain, and the chances are a thousand to one that our men would find nothing more than a few pickets to oppose them. In that way, instead of trying to drive back Banks' left wing and get behind his right wing, I'd pierce his center and get behind both wings." Doubtless General Jackson saw objections to such a move that were beyond the view of our able strategist.

Having finished their pipes, talked as long as they wished, and unanimously agreed that they would be in a fight before noon the next day, the men stretched themselves on the ground near their guns, and slept as peacefully as if there were no such thing as war in the world.

Buoyant with the excitement of expected battle, they were moving towards the enemy at an early hour next morning; but delay after delay occurred, and it was several hours past noon before a gun was fired. Taken completely by surprise, the enemy made but a feeble resistance. The only fighting worthy of mention was between Marylanders. The first Maryland regiment of Confederates, which was in advance, found the first Maryland regiment of Federals drawn up to oppose it. A telling volley from the Confederates, followed by an impetuous charge, caused the Federals to retreat in confusion. The rest of the Federal force followed their example. Many were captured, but most of them hurried away towards Winchester, pursued by our troops. They left behind them a great quantity of stores of various kinds, among them many edibles most tempting to a hungry man; but we had no time to stop for anything. And I think that not a man of us wanted to stop; for we could now see as clearly as General Jackson himself that the all-important thing was to hurry forward and head off the Federals by getting between them and Winchester.

Passing rapidly through the town, we pressed on in the wake of the retreating enemy until we came to Cedarville, where a crossroad branched off towards the main Valley turnpike, and were there halted. We had then made an ordinary day's march, but the men were eager to go on notwithstanding their weariness. The history that says the exhaustion of the men delayed the march until morning was, I think, written to excuse General Jackson's failure to get completely behind Banks, rather than to state the facts in the case. It is true that the men were tired, but they were ready and eager to go on; and certainly General Jackson did not stop because his men were tired on other occasions. It must have been for reasons other than the exhaustion of the men that "the march was delayed until morning."

My memory is not clear as to the hour when we left Cedarville next day; but it must have been late in the afternoon, as we did not reach the Valley turnpike, eight or ten miles away, until after dark. We came to the turnpike not far from Middletown, about halfway between Strasburg and Winchester, and found that the enemy had retreated more swiftly than we had advanced. General Banks had been quickly informed of the attack on Front Royal, and had lost no time in getting away from Strasburg. Before we reached the turnpike, his main body had passed on towards Winchester. A part of our troops, however, consisting of cavalry and artillery, had been in time to cut his column, and drive the rear end of it back towards Strasburg, The front had made no effort to aid the rear, it being a case of "devil take the hindmost."

Too late to intercept the retreating Federals, we stacked our arms alongside the road, and, lying down near them, were soon "dead to the world." When we had slept for what seemed to me not more than ten minutes, but was really about three hours, we were roused up and started on the road to Winchester. The short sleep I had got, instead of freshening me, made me more sleepy. Again and again, I went fast asleep while walking along, and waked myself falling, as one who nods is awakened by the dropping of his head. Determined not to join the stragglers, I wearily staggered on. Presently the eastern sky grew rosy with the dawn, but I barely noticed it. The rising sun bathed the summit of the distant Blue Ridge in splendor, but my eyes were too heavy to appreciate its beauty. Then came the boom of a cannon in our front, and at once I was wide-awake. The cannon shots followed one another in quick succession, and soon the rattle of musketry was heard. The rear guard of the Federals had made a stand just south of Winchester, and our troops were attacking. Away off on the right, the regiments that had come by the Front Royal road were gallantly charging; and on the left, regiments that had come down the valley pike ahead of us were pressing forward no less gallantly. Our weariness was all gone now, and we stepped as briskly as young athletes just starting in a race. The Federals, cowed and whipped ere the battle began, gave way before the impetuous advance of the Confederates, and fled in disorder. We were barely in time to join in chasing them through the streets of Winchester.

The people of that loyal Southern city, regardless of danger, rushed out to welcome us. Old men moved with a livelier step, threw their hats in the air, and lustily cheered. Boys shouted. Ladies, old and young, waved their handkerchiefs, threw kisses at the soldiers who were fighting for the cause they loved, and with enthusiastic demonstrations of gladness joined in the fervent greeting. Some were laughing, and some were moved to tears by their elation. The whole town seemed wild with joy. It was more than enough to banish fatigue. It was like strong wine to sluggish blood.

About five miles beyond Winchester, we were halted, and the cavalry took up the pursuit of the Federals. After resting a day or two and getting a fresh supply of rations taken from the captured store, we moved on to the Potomac. When we bivouacked near Harper's Ferry, where we did our first soldiering, General Banks with the remnant of his army, had crossed into Maryland, and was offering up thanks for his escape. He said in his report: "There never were more grateful hearts in the same number of men, than when...we stood on the opposite shore."

"Stonewall" Jackson
Valentine Museum

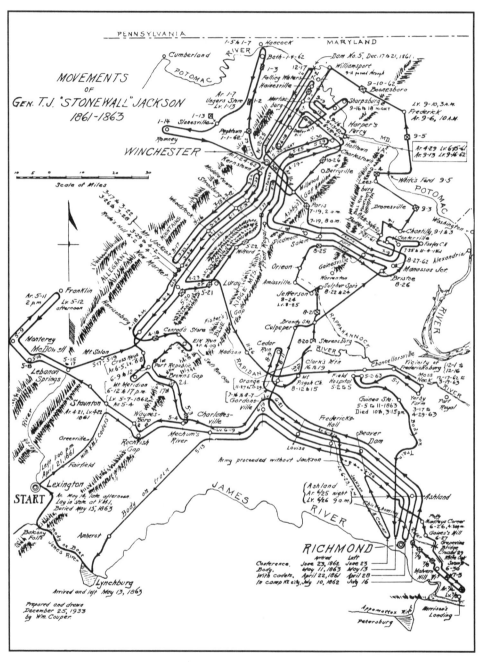

Map showing all of "Stonewall" Jackson's movements.
Compliments of
the Shenandoah Valley Civil War Roundtable

CHAPTER II

Defeating Generals John Fremont and James Shields

Although General Jackson was, for a time, in command of the troops at Harper's Ferry when we were there in the spring of 1861, I got only a distant glimpse of him then. I really saw him for the first time when, attended by several officers, he passed our bivouac, and stopped for some minutes on a near-by hill overlooking the Potomac, across which had flown the bird he had tried to bag.

His appearance did not impress me as extraordinary. While he did not have the splendid physique, courtly bearing, and gracious manner of General R. E. Lee, he did not strike me as remarkably ungainly in figure, awkward in movement, or rough in demeanor. He did not sit his horse with the easy, graceful, and elegant poise of General Stuart, but he was not uncommonly slouching in the saddle. I did not notice that his uniform looked older and more dingy than those worn by others, or that it bore evidence in accumulated dirt of having been oftener "slept in on the bare ground." His military cap did not appear to be conspicuously "old" and "yellowed," and I did not remark that it was tilted so far forward that he had to "lift his chin in the air to look under the brim." He did not have an "abstracted" and "absent-looking" air; he was not moving his lips as if "wrestling in prayer"; he made no imploring gesture with his hand, as if beckoning Heaven to his aid; and he was not "sucking a lemon." Neither then nor afterwards did I notice the remarkable peculiarities of figure, dress, manner, and habit ascribed to him by some

7

writers in their attempt to make him appear different from other men, and give him the earmarks of genius. To my mind, some of the oddities they attribute to him are suggestive of clownishness and crankiness rather than genius. I am glad that I can remember him without associating him with personal characteristics that really detract from his greatness; and, thus remembering him, I return to my story.

I think it was about ten o'clock on the morning of May 30th that we left the vicinity of Harper's Ferry and "took the back track." We were not usually told where we were going, when we started on a march; but on that occasion word was passed down the line from some source that our destination was Strasburg. Probably to incite us to "put the best foot foremost," it was said that two large Federal armies—one from the east and one from the west—were rapidly moving to form a junction in our rear; and that, if we didn't want to be caught in the trap, we would have to show ourselves to be "foot cavalry" in fact as well as in name, and get to Strasburg ahead of them.

Naturally this news gave rise to much talk among the men, and various opinions were expressed as to how long it would take us to get to Strasburg, and what would be the consequences of failure to get there ahead of the enemy.

"How far is it to Strasburg?" asked one.

"It can't be less than forty-five miles," was the answer.

"Well," said the first speaker, "we can make three miles an hour and get there by two o'clock in the morning, if 'old Jack' wants us to do it; but I wish he didn't want us to go back at all."

"You don't want to stay here and let the Yankees get in behind us, do you?" he was asked.

"Why should we worry about the Yankees getting behind us?" he questioned in reply. "If they get behind us, won't we get behind them? And ain't that just where we've been nearly marching our legs off to get ever since we left Luray?" This caused a general laugh, and the speaker continued: "If they should get behind us and shut us off from the South, the North would be open to us; and, if we were to cross the Potomac and invade Maryland and Pennsylvania, we would scare the whole Yankee nation nearly to death. Old Abe would call in half the men of their armies to defend Washington and keep us from capturing him; and all their well laid plans would be 'knocked into a cocked hat.' And up among the Pennsylvania Dutch, we'd have the time of our lives. What a lark it would be! I wish 'old Jack' would take us on it."

"So do I," was heard in a dozen different voices.

"But wouldn't they catch us?" someone asked.

"Possibly they would in the end," he replied, "but we could make it a long, hard job for them; and, before they could do it, we would have lots of fun, and probably accomplish more for the South than we can ever do by outmarching them to Strasburg and keeping ourselves out of prison."

Of course, this was mere badinage, but it expressed a feeling which, I think, was very general among the soldiers. I believe the army would have welcomed a forward movement, regardless of any force gathering behind us. It has been said that General Jackson himself had a leaning in that direction, and might have attempted such a movement, but for the fact that he wished to take out of the enemy's reach the several thousand prisoners and the great quantities of stores that had been captured from General Banks and were being collected in Winchester. These stores of various kinds were said to be worth over two millions of dollars, and it took a train of wagons twelve miles long to remove them. Jackson didn't want Fremont and Shields to recapture them, and was depending upon his "foot cavalry" to prevent it.

Dropping talk, with the exception of a brief comment or jesting remark now and then, we settled down to the work before us. It was tramp, tramp, tramp, throughout the day and far into the night, with an occasional halt of ten minutes for rest. Some time after dark, we passed through Winchester, and by eleven o'clock that night were within ten miles of Strasburg. I suppose those in command then knew that we had outmarched the Federals; for the column was halted, arms were stacked, and we were told that we would spend the rest of the night there.

Lying on the bare ground, some of us using our cartridge-boxes for pillows, others pillowing their brows on their folded arms, and others still stretched on their backs with their heads on a level with their bodies, we were soon taking "sore labor's bath" and "tired nature's sweet restorer."

My aching muscles kept me awake for a little while, but my right hand comrade was quickly asleep. Presently I heard him mutter: "I must go—Virginia needs me"; and a moment later: "Kiss me good-bye, mother—don't grieve—I'll be back soon." His tired eyes had scarcely closed in slumber before his spirit, borne of the wings of a dream, was back in his dear Old Virginia home, and in the presence of the devoted mother whom he loved most fervently, and whose prayers were ever going up to heaven for him. In his dream, he was leaving home in response to the call of his country; the sweet and gentle face of his mother was before him; he saw the tears which she struggled to keep back gathering in her eyes as she kissed him good-bye; and was trying to cheer her with the hope that he would soon be with her again. Alas! In less than a month after that dream of home and mother and going back to them, his bullet-torn body was cold and still on the battle ground near Richmond, and his brave, loyal, and loving soul had winged its way to God.

At three o'clock we were roused and, refreshed by four hours of sleep, started on the home-stretch. Strasburg was reached a little before seven o'clock. General Fremont, coming from the west by the Romney road, was then within four or five miles of the town, and we moved out to front him and hold him in check. The story, told in some of the histories, that General Ewell attacked and drove back Fremont's advance force, has no foundation in fact. During the day, a few dozen shots were exchanged between us and the skirmish line in the enemy's front, but there was no attack and no battle. Where we were, there was no line of battle. We were deployed as skirmishers, at least ten paces apart, to present an extended front, and make a show of strength which we did not have. General Fremont, it was said, had an army of more than twenty thousand men; and any competent commander in his place would have soon found out how weak we were, and, running over us without a halt, would have cut off Jackson's retreat. But there he kept his large army all day long, afraid to make any move, held back by nothing more than our line of widely separated skirmishers, while the prisoners captured from Banks, the long train of wagons loaded with the spoils of war, and the main body of Jackson's army were passing through Strasburg behind us. General Jackson's escape with the prisoners and stores was due to the utter incompetency of the Federal commander.

About sunset, the last of our troops reached Strasburg, and Jackson was entirely clear of the trap in which the enemy thought to catch him. Quietly withdrawing from Fremont's front, we followed the main body of the army up the Valley. I think it was not until next day that the Federal commander mustered up courage enough to move in pursuit. Then he came on behind us, his cavalry skirmishing, now and then, with Ashby's troopers.

Near Woodstock, the Federal cavalry made a sudden and dashing attack on some of our cavalrymen, who, wholly unprepared to meet the onslaught, fell back in such haste and disorder that they ran into and greatly confused a regiment of the 2nd Brigade of infantry, under Colonel Patton, which was then marching in the rear of our column. The infantry, however, were quickly rallied, and, forming on each side of the road, poured into the advancing Federals a volley that drove them back with considerable loss. But three of these Federal cavalrymen, instead of turning back with their troop, fearlessly charged on through the brigade. Two of them were killed, but the other miraculously escaped.

In connection with this affair, one of General Jackson's biographers relates a story of him which I am loath to believe, because it is altogether inconsistent with his reputation as a humane and Christian man. As the writer tells it, Colonel Patton, in reporting the matter, expressed admiration for the three daring men, and said that, if he had been able, he would have prevented the troops from firing on them. "Why would you not have shot those men, Colonel?" Jackson curtly asked. "I should have spared them, General," returned the officer, "because they were brave men who had gotten into a desperate situation where it was as easy to capture them as to kill them." Jackson coldly said: "Shoot them all; I don't want them to be brave." I cannot think that Jackson, a civilized and Christian man, wished his soldiers to kill those whom they could as easily capture; and I class this story with others in which writers have grossly misrepresented him in their mistaken attempts to make him seem a peculiar genius.

Soon after this affair, we crossed the Shenandoah a few miles south of Mount Jackson, and destroyed the bridge over that river. This delayed Fremont's advance, and our rear was not again molested while we were moving up the Valley.

Just beyond Harrisonburg, we left the Valley turnpike, and proceeded along a country road to Port Republic. There Jackson halted, with the design of striking in detail Fremont, who was following him, and Shields, who was advancing through the Luray Valley. I shall not attempt to give a full account of how he did this. Suffice it to say that, while he proceeded with his own division to Port Republic, he left our division near Cross Keys, some miles out on the Harrisonburg road, to await the arrival of Fremont. That General advanced in force and attacked us on the 8th of June, and was defeated in what is known as the battle of Cross Keys. That night, leaving a small force to resist any further forward movement that Fremont might attempt, General Ewell moved us to Port Republic, where we joined the main body of the army and took part in the battle with the force under General Shields next day.

Either because they had a better commander or because they were better men, the soldiers of Shields put up a much more stubborn fight than did those of Fremont. The battle of Port Republic was one of the fiercest and, considering the numbers engaged, one of the bloodiest of the War between the States; but, after desperate fighting and heavy loss, our troops succeeded in driving the Federals back down the Luray Valley.

The battle of Port Republic closed the famous Valley campaign—a campaign which, in brilliant and daring strategy, in rapidity of movement, in the courage and endurance of the soldiers, and in the magnitude of results for the size of the army, is almost without a parallel in military history.

After the battle, when the troops were bivouacked for the night, one of my messmates, who was seated on a log with his shoes in his hands and solemnly contemplating their worn soles, suddenly exclaimed:

"It's a d——d misnomer."

"What're you talking about? Do you mean it's a misnomer to call those things shoes?" he was asked.

"No," he replied. "I mean the name they've given Old Jack is a misnomer. Why, they call him Stonewall, and they might just as well call these rusty old brogans patent leather pumps. A stone wall never moves around, and he's always moving around. Look at these shoes. Three weeks ago they were bran-new, with soles an inch thick that I thought I could never wear out. Now see. I've worn them clean through the inside soles, following him around. And I'll bet all I've got, down to the ragged and dirty shirt on my back, that he'll have us footing it again before I have time to get another pair. He's no stone wall; he's a lion on the jump for prey. Stonewall? Pshaw! It's a d——d misnomer; that's what it is."

CHAPTER III

The Seven Days' Battle

What is called the Seven Days' Battle was a series of battle and skirmishes, beginning on the 26th of June and ending on the 2nd of July. Of the army then threatening Richmond, a force of about 25,000 men, commanded by General Fitz John Porter, was on the north side of the Chickahominy River; and the plan of General Lee was to drive back and, if possible, destroy this force, seize General McClellan's line of communication with his base of operations, and thus compel him to retreat as best he could. To carry out this plan, troops already near Richmond were to strongly attack the Federals in front, and Jackson, arriving from the Valley, was to simultaneously swoop down on their right flank and rear.

To perform their part of this program, the troops under Jackson were moved on towards Richmond, and, on the evening of June 25th, reached a station on what was then the Virginia Central railroad, some eight or ten miles from that city, where they bivouacked for the night. The next morning—the day on which the attack was to be made—they moved in an easterly direction towards the scene of the coming conflict; but, for some unexplained reason, their start was not as early as it might have been and their progress was slower than usual, so that they were late in reaching their designated position.

The statement that Jackson was late in getting into position because his men were fatigued by previous long marches and he was unexpectedly delayed by the enemy has little foundation in fact. It is true that the men had been marching every day for more than a week; but they had been marching by comparatively easy stages, their strength has not been overtaxed, and they were far from being exhausted. It is also true that they came upon some small detachments of the enemy; but no delay of consequence was caused thereby, as the Federals hastily retired before them. Whatever may have been the cause of Jackson's tardiness on that occasion, it was neither the weariness of his troops nor any formidable opposition by the enemy.

It was about five o'clock in the afternoon when the column was halted at a place called Hundley's Corner. While lying there, the men distinctly heard the sounds of battle off to the right and apparently not more than a mile or two away. They commented on the heavy firing, and noted that the sound of it continued to come from the same direction, which indicated that the Federals were stubbornly holding their ground. Some of them wondered why they were not pushed forward to aid the attacking Confederates and turn the tide of battle; but all thought it must be for some good reason. The unanimous opinion was: "Old Jack knows what he's about, and it's all right."

But later, when they learned that General A. P. Hill had vainly endeavored to dislodge the Federals from their position on Beaver Dam Creek and thought of how his success would have changed the whole situation, they freely said that, whoever was responsible for it, the failure to go to his aid was a great mistake.

As I have intimated before, these Confederate privates did not concede to their generals a monopoly of military judgment. They did a lot of thinking for themselves, and they were not overly backward in stating their views of what had been and ought to be done. Some of them said that, if we had gone to Hill's aid by attacking the Federals in flank and rear, as we were in a position to do, they would have been easily driven back and, if closely pursued, would have been unable to take another stand north of the Chickahominy. And I think they were not far wrong. I believe that, with the prompt and vigorous cooperation of Jackson, the Federal force on the north side of the Chickahominy could have been shattered on the afternoon and evening of June 26th, and we could have cut McClellan off from his base of operations and threatened his line of retreat without fighting the terribly fierce and bloody battle of the next day.

But somebody blundered; and the next day found the enemy occupying a strong position near Gaines' Mill, heavily reinforced, and thoroughly prepared to give battle. General Long, who was then the military secretary of General Lee, says: "The Federal position near Gaines' Mill was a plateau bounded on the north-west

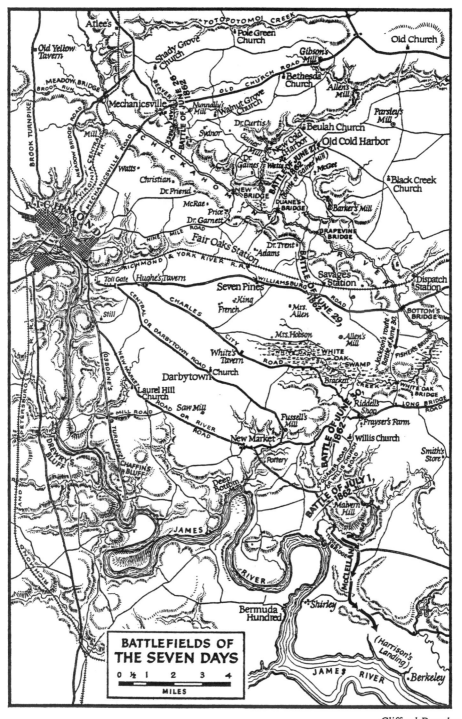

BATTLEFIELDS OF
THE SEVEN DAYS

0 ½ 1 2 3 4
MILES

Clifford Dowdey

side by a bluff eighty or ninety feet in elevation, which, curving to the north and east, gradually diminished into a gentle slope. The plateau was bounded on the north side by a stream flowing along its base, whose banks gradually widened and deepened until, when reaching the bluff, they had gained the width of eight or ten and the depth of five or six feet, thus forming a natural ditch. Three lines of breastworks, rising one above the other, had been constructed upon the base of the bluff, and its crest was crowned with artillery. Three lines of Federal infantry occupied the bluff, and one line extended along the north-east crest for more than a mile, and batteries of artillery were in position in rear of the infantry.

On the morning of June 27th, the Confederates moved forward to attack this strong position in three columns—Longstreet on the right, A. P. Hill in the center, and Jackson on the left. Owing, it was said, to indefinite instructions given by Jackson to his guide, his column took the wrong road, ran into the division of Hill, had to countermarch to gain the right road, and did not reach the scene of conflict until some time after the troops of Hill and Longstreet had become hotly engaged. When it arrived, our brigade, commanded by General Elzey, was sent to the support of Hill.

For at least two hours the battle raged fiercely without any visible weakening of the Federal lines. At several points, the Confederates attempted to force them and were repulsed with heavy loss. Finally, a general charge was ordered, and, with a wild "rebel yell," the whole Confederate line swept forward. There was no thought of alignment; only a determined dash for the enemy. The charging men were met by a terrific fire from the guns on the crest of the hill. The three lines of Federal infantry in the tiers of breastworks on the face of the bluff threw a murderous hail of bullets into their ranks. The artillery fire cut great gaps in their line. But leaving the field behind them strewed with dead and wounded, the living and uninjured swept on with an irresistible rush. In a few minutes the whole position was taken, and the enemy was in full flight. History tells of no more gallant and intrepid charge—no greater display of dauntless courage and heroic resolution. When the strength of their position is considered, it seems almost incredible that the Federals, who were about equal to their assailants in numerical strength, were driven from it by a front attack.

If there were any skulkers in that fight, the men of Elzey's brigade were not among them. The losses of the regiments composing that brigade bear witness that they faced the deadliest fire of the enemy. My own company, which had lost half of its complement in the battles and marches of the campaign in the Valley, went into the fight with about fifty men. It came out with about fifteen, having lost II, including the Captain, killed and 24 wounded. I have no reason to think that the other companies of the brigade were exposed to a less deadly fire, and suppose they lost in about the same proportion. General Early, who took command of the brigade two or three days after the fight, says in his "Narrative" that he found it composed of mere "remnants of regiments."

On the morning of the 28th, our division was sent, in support of the cavalry, to seize the York River Railroad and cut McClellan off from his base of supplies. This was done without opposition; and we were then sent to Bottom's Bridge, farther down the Chickahominy, to guard against any attempt the Federals might make to cross to the north side of the river at that point. There we remained until the next day, when we rejoined Jackson, who had crossed to the south side of the river and was moving along the road to White Oak Swamp.

This road, like most others in the Chickahominy region, was in many places little more than a narrow wagon-track. Here it dipped into a lonely ravine that looked like a haunt of owls and wild beasts, and there it crossed a low ridge darkened by the thick foliage of great trees and tangled undergrowth. Then free of the forest, it often led across damp and soggy lowland, and over sluggish streams bordered by wide swamps and jungles. The retreating Federals had felled trees across it, destroyed the bridges over the streams, and done everything possible to impede our progress. Our march, therefore, was necessarily slow.

Reaching White Oak Swamp on the 30th, we found the bridge over the stream destroyed, and the enemy in force posted on the rising ground beyond, with artillery and infantry commanding the position and making the rebuilding of the bridge impossible.

While lying there, with the passage of the swamp before us completely blocked, we heard heavy firing a few miles off to our right; and, as it increased in volume and the sound continued to come from the same quarter, we became convinced that a fierce battle was raging, and that the Confederates badly needed help. As we learned later, it was the battle of Frazier's Farm, in which Hill and Longstreet vainly tried to take the position held by the force covering McClellan's retreat. Had their attack been successful, as it almost certainly would have been with the support of Jackson, it is more than probable, military experts say, that McClellan's entire army would have been destroyed. But, for some reason, Jackson's support was not given.

Commenting on the situation, one of my comrades said: "Old Jack don't seem to be living up to his Valley record since he came down to this region. These sluggish streams and stagnant pools and dismal swamps seem to have shaken his nerve. It isn't like the Jackson of the Valley to hold back when the sounds of battle call, and it seems to me that's just what he's doing now. In my opinion, those sounds loudly call him to the aid of our men; and <u>he</u> may see why we should be kept here doing nothing instead of going to help them, but I'll be damned if <u>I</u> can."

General Jackson was much blamed by some for his failure to go to the aid of Hill and Longstreet on that occasion, and he would probably have been blamed still more but for his brilliant achievements on other fields. His biographers, however, have stoutly defended his action. Colonel Henderson, of the British army, regarding all commands to follow a given course until further orders as foolish, says that Jackson, as strict in obedience as he was in exacting it, was merely obeying the foolish order of General Lee that he should proceed along the road leading through White Oak Swamp "until further orders." But, as a matter of fact, General Jackson was not carrying out that order—was not <u>proceeding</u> along the road leading through "White Oak Swamp." He had found the way so blocked that he could not proceed—could not carry out the order—and, as the lay mind reasons, it then became his duty to immediately report to his superior his inability to go forward, and to act on his own judgment until further instructions were received. But, instead of reporting his inability to advance and using his troops to the best advantage until General Lee could be heard from, he remained inactive on the flank of a position against which Hill and Longstreet were vainly hurling their troops, and the carrying of which was of the utmost importance.

It is said that, on being asked why he did not go to the support of the Confederates at Frazier's Farm, General Jackson curtly

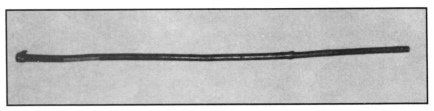

ARTIFACT FROM THE BATTLEFIELD AT SEVEN PINES
Inscribed on the walking cane pictured above is the following:
"Cut in the center of the Seven Pines Battlefield where 15,000 soldiers were killed May31st and June 1st 1862. Battle fought by Lee and McClellan. Battlefield guide. J. C. Lyne"
Author's Cane

answered: "If General Lee had wanted me he would have sent for me." General Lee would doubtless have done so, had he been informed of the true condition of things; but, as no report to the contrary was sent to him, he had every reason to suppose that Jackson was proceeding as directed, and thus doing just what was desired by getting in rear of the Federals and cutting off their retreat.

While Jackson's military genius is beyond question, I think it must be admitted that, in the fighting before Richmond, he twice failed to rise to the occasion, when by so doing he would have made the defeat of the Federals far more disastrous. General D. H. Hill has said that Jackson was never at his best when acting under the orders of a superior—that "the hooded falcon could not strike the quarry." Whether that be creditable to Jackson or otherwise, it may be true; for all his most brilliant feats were achieved when he was, to a large extent, free from the direction of a superior. In the battle of Cedar Run, or Slaughter's Mountain, in the movement around Pope to Manassas, in the capture of Harper's Ferry, and in turning the flank of Hooker at the battle of Chancellorsville, he was, if not so independent as he was in the Valley, temporarily detached and comparatively free to follow his own judgment. At Richmond, he seemed afraid to take the initiative and depart from the strict letter of his orders, when changed conditions demanded and would have more than justified such departure.

The Federals held their positions at White Oak Swamp and Frazier's Farm until nightfall, and then retired under cover of the darkness. The way being opened, we followed on, and came up with them again at Malvern Hill, where we found them in an admirably selected and almost impregnable position. This position was not attacked until nearly sundown, and the attack continued until after dark. The approaches to it, which would have been difficult by daylight, were such as to render a night attack well-nigh hopeless. In the darkness, it was impossible to avoid mistakes and consequent confusion.

The battle of Malvern Hill has been rightly described as "a desperate struggle against immense odds and a vast amount of heavy siege guns and field artillery." Notwithstanding the immense odds against the Confederates, I believe they would have succeeded in carrying the almost impregnable position but for the lack of concerted action. But, because of morasses and swamps passable at only a few places and forests with dense and tangled undergrowth impeding communication, the different sections of the Confederate line were to a large extent out of touch with one another, and, instead of a concerted attack, there were separate attacks, now here and then there, no one of which was strong enough to succeed. Even as it was, some of our brigades pushed up the hill until they gained ground occupied by the enemy, and held their advanced positions through the night. When morning dawned, it was found that our brigade, then commanded by General Early, and the brigades of Generals Wright and Mahone were lying close to the summit of the hill, with their own and the enemy's dead around them. The Confederates were ready to resume the fight, but the Federals had quietly retired during the night.

This was the last severe engagement of "The Seven Days' Battles." We followed the retreating Federals towards Harrison's Landing, and had some skirmishing with their rear guard, but there was no further fighting of consequence. General McClellan had succeeded in conducting his army to safety, and had inflicted heavy loss on his adversary in retiring. His army had been beaten, but it had not been routed and demoralized. I believe that, under the circumstances, no other Northern General could have done as well. Instead of regarding him as a failure, the North should build a monument to George B. McClellan, her greatest general.

C HAPTER IV

Battle of Cedar (Slaughter's) Mountain

The engagement with the advance of General Pope's army on the 9th of August, 1862, has been variously designated as the Battle of Slaughter's Mountain, the Battle of Cedar Mountain, and the Battle of Cedar Run. I call it the Battle Slaughter's Mountain, because it was so named by the soldiers at the time and has always been so called by the people of that region.

Slaughter's Mountain, six or seven miles southwest of Culpeper Courthouse, stands in the midst of a comparatively level country. For several miles north, south, and east of it, and out to the Culpeper road west of it, were gently undulating fields, some of them in cultivation. West of the road, extending along it for a considerable distance, was a large body of woods.

Our brigade, proceeding along that road at the head of the column, reached a point a little beyond the Mountain about eleven o'clock in the morning. The sound of brisk skirmishing ahead of us indicated that our cavalry was meeting with something more than the resistance of retreating raiders, and we were moved from the road into the woods on our left and halted to await developments. A passing courier whom we asked for news told us that a strong force of Federals was in position about two miles in front, and that a heavy column was coming up from the direction of Culpeper Courthouse.

We remained in the shelter of the woods until after two o'clock, when, Jackson's division having come up, we were moved forward a short distance and formed in line of battle along a low ridge almost

21

at right angles with the Culpeper road, Ewell's division being in the fields east of it and Jackson's in the woods west of it. My regiment formed the extreme left of Ewell's division, and Taliaferro's brigade was in the woods just across the road from us. The ground in our immediate front gently sloped down to a small stream about two hundred yards from our line, and then gradually rose for about the same distance to the plain beyond.

Our position was such that I saw more of that battle than of any other in which I took part. Ordinarily a private soldier sees nothing of a fight in which he is engaged except what takes place directly in front of him and within a few yards to the right and left of him. But from where my regiment was posted in this engagement the whole stretch of open country in Ewell's front—one half of the battle-ground—was in plain view, and one could also see the larger part of a field which, taking in both sides of the small stream I have mentioned, extended nearly half a mile in front of the woods held by Taliaferro's brigade. I plainly saw, and still clearly visualize, incidents of that battle which took place fully a mile from where I was.

When our line was formed, instead of being ordered to advance and attack the enemy as we were expecting to be, we were told to lie down just below the crest of the ridge. It has been said that the Federals were defeated in that battle because they were attacked by Jackson with overwhelming numbers before they got all their force on the field; but this statement is refuted by the fact that Jackson did not make the attack. The attack was made by the Federals when Jackson's full force was not up—when he had only two divisions in position and was waiting for A. P. Hill to arrive. They opened the battle with a fierce artillery fire, which they kept up for about two hours, but which did us little damage, as we were partially protected by the nature of the ground and the aim of their gunners was decidedly poor. Most of their shot went high over us. I heard of only one man in my regiment who was hurt, and he was slightly wounded by the fragment of a shell that burst more than a hundred feet up in the air. Instead of being demoralized by this cannonade, as the enemy hoped, our men were wholly indifferent to it. In fact, some of them were lulled to sleep by the monotonous booming of the guns.

About five o'clock, when we were supposed to be somewhat demoralized by the artillery fire, there appeared on the far side of the plain before us a line of the enemy's infantry which confronted the whole of Ewell's division and extended into the woods west of the road. A few minutes later, another line of apparently equal length came into view following the first. We could see them for at least ten minutes before they got within musket range, coming on in magnificent

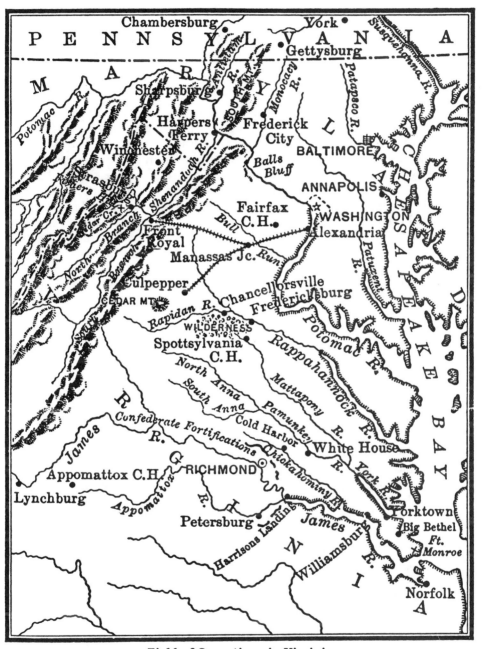

Field of Operations in Virginia

style through a field of young corn and seemingly aligned as perfectly as if they were on dress parade. The sight reminded me of exhibition drills given by crack regiments, only it was on a vaster scale. From where these glittering lines of bayonets began on our extreme right to where they disappeared in the woods off to our left seemed to me at least a mile and a half.

The thought that we had but one thin line of battle to meet these thousands backed by thousands steadily moving towards us and about to hurl themselves upon us was not cheering; but, if the men around me were discouraged by the prospect, they did not show it. Looking on them, I saw determination in their faces and the light of battle shining in their eyes, as it had shone there when they charged to victory across the bloody field of Cold Harbor. I saw that their hands did not tremble as, without waiting for orders, they loosed the flaps of their cartridge boxes, examined the caps on their muskets, and prepared to receive the shock that was coming. I felt that with such men we might win, in spite of what seemed to be overwhelming odds against us.

When the Federals came within musket range, but were still distant, a shimmering wave of light flashed along their line as their guns, reflecting the rays of the sun, were shifted into position for firing; innumerable puffs of smoke, blending into a long strip of cloud, shot out before them; and, in an instant, bullets were zip-zip-zipping about the ears of our men and here and there finding lodgment in the body of a gray-clad soldier. The guns all along the Confederate line rattled and roared in reply, sending a deadly hail of lead into their ranks; but steadily and bravely they came on, firing as they advanced.

As they were rushing down the slope of the little hill opposite our line, a battery that had been doing splendid work from a position just in advance of the centre of our brigade limbered up and galloped to the rear to escape capture. Its retreat seemed to cause a panic among the men near it, and several regiments fell back in confusion, leaving a gap in our line more than half a mile wide, on the other side of which I saw the troops on Ewell's extreme right still gallantly holding their ground.

At the same time, as we learned a few minutes later, the troops of Jackson's division were faring badly. The enemy, under cover of the woods, had thrown a heavy column around their left which, assailing them in flank and rear, had forced them back with grievous loss. Taliaferro's brigade, which, as I have said, was just across the road from us, and which had courageously held its ground against the force attacking it in front, was rolled back and driven from the field by the attack on its flank, leaving our left completely exposed.

The situation at that time may be summed up thus: West of the road, the whole Confederate line had been driven back on Winder's brigade, which had been held in reserve and was fiercely fighting to stay the onward rush of the foe. East of the road, the centre of Ewell's division had been driven back, leaving in line a few regiments still bravely battling on his extreme right and our regiment alone, with both flanks unprotected, on his left. No reinforcements were in sight, and the battle seemed irretrievably lost.

Then there was an exhibition of courage and determination by the men of my regiment (the 13th Virginia Infantry) such as would have done credit to the Old Guard of Napoleon—such as was not excelled by the men of the Light Brigade, who charged while

> Cannon to right of them,
> Cannon to left of them,
> Cannon in front of them
> Volley'd and thunder'd.

Above the noise of the battle rose the deep, powerful voice of our Colonel, shouting: "Men of the 13th, F-o-r-w-a-r-d." The command surprised and startled me, for I saw that we were in an extremely dangerous position and was rather eagerly expecting an order to fall back. The thought flashed through my mind that Colonel Walker intended to sacrifice himself and his regiment in the hope of checking the enemy's advance long enough for the officers to rally the men who had been driven from the field. Apparently, a forward movement meant death or captivity for himself and every man of his command. But the men did not hesitate.

> Theirs not to reason why,
> Theirs but to do and die,

if duty called them to death. I was told that General Ewell, sweeping the field with his glasses from his station on the mountain and seeing the advance of these men, said: "I duly honor the famous Stonewall Brigade, but give me four regiments like that going forward yonder and I will form an iron brigade that would storm the battlements of hell."

There was no shouting as the regiment advanced—no "rebel yell" such as was born of the excitement and enthusiasm of charging thousands confident of victory. With an unopposed enemy pressing on to sweep around their right, and their left already under fire from the Federals who had driven back the brigade of Taliaferro, silently, steadily, sternly, determined to die if necessary, but to sell their lives as dearly as possible, the men moved forward to meet the foe advancing in their front. An officer from Taliaferro's brigade, hatless, coatless, the front of his shirt torn open, and his face and bare bosom begrimed with dust and sweat, dashed up behind their flag and, waving his sword, shouted: "My men have left me, but I'm going on with you boys."

Passing over the crest of the ridge, they poured into the Federals, who had reached the little stream in the bottom and were in easy pistol range, a fire that rapidly thinned their line. In less time than it takes to tell of it, the north bank of that little stream was thickly strewed with the dead and dying. The enemy's line directly in our front was shattered. It seemed to me that almost half of it went down. The rest retreated in disorder.

This forward movement and terrific fire checked the advance of the Federals in our front, but with both of our flanks exposed our position was untenable. A courier galloped up with orders for Colonel Walker to fall back and save his regiment from capture. Under a flanking fire from the Federals who had taken Taliaferro's position, the men retired slowly and without the slightest sign of disorder.

As we moved back, an officer who was a few paces in front of me fell forward on his face, spasmodically raised his body from the ground on his elbows and toes, held it thus raised for a moment, and then collapsed in death without a groan. A bullet had pierced his brain.

When we had gone back about three hundred yards, we saw a brigade of Hill's division, which had just arrived, advancing in line of battle west of the road. Then the regiment threw discipline to the winds. Without waiting for orders, the men faced about and again started for the enemy; and before this advance, which quickly extended along our whole line, the Federals everywhere gave way.

We dashed forward in pursuit of the fleeing foe, giving no thought to alinement [sic]. In some way it chanced that thirty or forty of us got considerably in advance of the body of the regiment; and, when we reached the little stream where so many Federal dead were lying, we saw the head of a column of cavalry coming over the crest of the hill before us and swiftly bearing down upon us. Gallantly the cavalry came on, in column of fours, at full gallop, their empty scabbards jangling, their bare sabers flashing. Being ahead of the regiment, we had no officer with us; and the only command I heard was given by a private from Orange who said: "Here come the devils who've been raiding our homes. Send them where they belong." Moved by a common impulse, the men closed up and braced themselves for the coming shock. They reserved their fire until the head of the column was within fifteen or twenty paces of them. Then their guns spoke almost as one, and fully a dozen saddles were emptied. The officer leading the charge, who seemed to lose control of his frightened horse, swerved to the right and, circling through the field west of the road, went back at full speed. The column followed its leader. As it circled back, it was exposed to the fire of the brigade of Hill's division, which was coming down the slope on our left and rear, and the path of its retreat was marked by dead horses and brave men who would never charge again.

Thus the Battle of Slaughter's Mountain, which at one time seemed about to result in the disastrous defeat of the Confederates, ended in a complete Confederate victory. And I believe that to the 13th. Virginia Infantry justly belongs the honor of saving the day. Had that regiment retreated with the troops that gave way on both sides of it, there would have been nothing to hinder the entire Federal centre from sweeping across the field, wheeling to right and left, assailing both the remaining regiment of Ewell and the newly arrived troops of Hill in flank and rear, and utterly routing the Confederate forces. The cool judgment and quick decision of Colonel (afterwards General) Walker, who took in the situation and ordered his regiment forward, prevented that. Bravely standing alone, with both flanks exposed and no aid in sight, and boldly moving forward at the critical moment, that heroic regiment guarded the Confederate centre and checked the enemy's advance long enough for Ewell's broken troops to be reformed and Hill's division to come into action without being subjected to an enfilading fire.

CHAPTER V

Back to Manassas

Early next morning, August 25th, we crossed the river and took a road leading in a northwesterly direction. We had no idea of where we were going; but all the indications led us to believe we were in for a long and strenuous forward movement. So, throwing away whatever we had in the way of needless impedimenta, we fell into our "Valley stride"—the steady, swinging gait with which we had won the cognomen of "foot cavalry."

We had not gone far when we saw General Lee, on the veranda of a house that stood close to the road and looked like it had once been a store. I had never before seen him at short range, and this near view of him excited my highest admiration. "He's a born king of men," I said to the comrade next to me. "I've seen handsomer faces, but never a nobler one; and, taken altogether, I never saw a finer-looking man." He was standing at the time—his head bared, his left arm bent at the elbow and holding his hat just in front of him, his right arm at his side, his splendid and perfectly proportioned figure graceful in every outline and poise. Having observed that, in army life, officers as well as privates generally yielded to the temptation to become somewhat slovenly, I noted with some surprise his perfect neatness. He seemed thoroughly well-groomed and clean. From his head, crowned with silvered hair that looked as if it had just received the finishing touches of a barber, to his feet, remarkably small for a man of his size and incased in neatly fitting and highly polished boots, there was nothing unkempt about him.

But what impressed me most deeply was not his physical perfection and exceptional neatness, but the moral qualities indicated by his appearance. The whole aspect of the man spoke of moral cleanness, spiritual purity, and knightly nobility. As he looked down on the ragged, poorly fed, but courageous men sturdily marching by to bravely face death on the field of battle, his eyes were gentle, tender, even loving, and his face beamed with benevolence and pity. It was a face that invited confidence and challenged implicit trust. One felt certain that the man with those eyes and that face could never knowingly do an unjust, ungenerous, or unkind thing. There came to me the thought that, in a time of trouble, one could go to him as a child to its parents and be as sure of finding sympathy. From that hour to this, I have thought of him as the knightliest gentleman who ever graced the American Continent, given him the loyalty and devotion of a soldier to an honored and heroic leader, and loved him with something like the purest and warmest filial affection.

I noticed that the soldiers did not greet him with cheers as they were wont to greet General Jackson. This, I think, was not because they honored him less, but because his presence awakened within them an entirely different feeling—a feeling that was too deep to find expression in noisy demonstrations and revealed itself in respectful and reverential silence. I cannot say how it was with others, but his presence awakened in me a feeling closely akin to worship—a feeling such as steals over one when he contemplates the sublime and sees in it a revelation of the Divine Majesty. This may seem extravagant; but, if so, I trust it is an extravagance that may be permitted to one who thinks Robert Edward Lee was a manifestation of the Divine such as is rarely vouchsafed unto men.

For some time after starting on this northward march, we heard the booming of guns in the direction of Jeffersonton, and conjectured (rightly as the event proved) that General Longstreet was vigorously bombarding the Federals across the river, for the purpose of keeping their attention so fixed upon their front that they would not observe our movement around their flank.

As we proceeded, the sounds and sights of war diminished, and the country took on a more peaceful appearance. The section through which we passed, being off the main line of travel, had not, up to that time, been visited by a large body of troops from either army, and no devastating hand had been laid upon it. Its stretches of woodland and its fields of grass and corn, freshened and beautified by the recent rain, were restful to our eyes. Its pretty farmhouses, set in shady groves back from the road and surrounded by smooth lawns ornamented with vines and flowers, made us dream of home and the happy days before war came with its blood and tears and desolations.

The heat became oppressive as the August sun mounted higher in the heavens; but fortunately the road, though dry enough to be firm, was not dusty, and we did not have to inhale powdered dirt with the air we breathed. Although the march was a trying one, there were few stragglers. Not knowing where they were going, but knowing they had passed the enemy's front and thinking they might be needed for action at any moment, the men stuck to their places in the ranks in spite of fatigue. I think this was characteristic of that army. The men were much given to straggling when they knew that no enemy was near and thought it could make little difference whether they were in the ranks or not, but I believe no army ever had a smaller percentage of stragglers when a battle was imminent.

Evening found us near Salem, a village on the Manassas Gap Railroad, about twenty-five miles west of Manassas Junction. There we bivouacked for the night. By that time, we privates had got a fairly correct idea of our destination. We were confident that a long march was before us on the next day, and that we would spend the next night somewhere on the Orange and Alexandria Railroad, directly in the rear of General Pope's army.

Just before dark, a courier came from General Early with a message to our Colonel, and raised a laugh by telling us how he had that afternoon heard the customary order to "fall in" improved upon by Colonel Smith of the 49th. Virginia Infantry—formerly Governor William Smith whom his friends familiarly called "Extra Billy." On the march, the column was halted occasionally to give the men a chance to break ranks and enjoy a short rest. As the courier told it, he was riding by the regiment just as the time for rest was up, and heard the Colonel order the men to "fall in." Being very tired, they didn't get up promptly, and the Colonel again, and with greater emphasis, commanded: "Fall in, forty-ninth." Many of the men still remained on the ground, wishing to steal another minute of rest, and Colonel Smith, losing patience, rose in his stirrups and shouted at the top of his voice: "Fall in forty-ninth, or I'll march the regiment off and leave every d——d one of you here." This was effective. The men jumped to their feet, at some one's suggestion gave three cheers for "Extra Billy," and hilariously took their places in the ranks.

We were roused from slumber before dawn next morning, and sunrise found us on the road leading eastward. Passing through Thoroughfare Gap in the Bull Run Mountains and going by the village of Gainesville on the Warrenton turnpike, we reached Bristoe Station, on the Orange and Alexandria Railroad, late in the afternoon.

We had marched more than fifty miles in two days, and were then a little over twenty miles from where we started, and about fifteen miles in rear of the Federal army. A detachment was sent that night to take possession of Manassas Junction, which was six or seven miles farther north and the chief depot of Pope's supplies. The other two divisions of our corps moved on to Manassas early next morning, leaving our division at Bristoe to retard the advance of any force that might be sent against us.

We did not have to wait many hours for the appearance of the enemy. General Pope, who in his bombastic address to his army had spoken with thinly veiled contempt of those who considered "lines of retreat and bases of supplies," was moved to consider such things himself, when he learned that, instead of "lying off on the flanks of the rebels," as he had boastfully declared he would do, he had permitted them to get around his flank, cut his line of communication, and capture his supplies. His position on the Rappahannock being no longer tenable, he hastily abandoned it, and hurried his army back to attack the enemy in his rear. The advance brigades of his column, which reached Bristoe early that afternoon, were easily repulsed by our division; but others, and more of them, advanced, and it soon became evident that an overwhelming force was opposed to us. Making a show of strength to check them—a show of strength that made them cautious and kept them from proceeding beyond Bristoe that night—General Ewell withdrew his division to Manassas.

At Manassas, we found the men of the other divisions feasting on good things intended for the enemy, and gladly joined them. It was a change from short rations to overflowing abundance. The Washington Government provided for its soldiers bountifully. Such another collection of supplies of every kind, I never saw. What specially interested us, however, was the supply of things to eat and drink. There were sutler's stores of choice liquors, fruits, and delicacies; great quantities of sugar and coffee; carloads of meat and flour; and a profusion of everything included in the rations of well-fed soldiers. The liquors were guarded and dealt out gingerly, lest some of us should imbibe too freely and become unfit for duty; but we had unrestrained access to everything else, and indulged our appetites to satiety. My friend Bogue, who had a great fondness for good things to eat, was happy. He said he would be glad to stay there for weeks, with nothing to do but eat, drink, sleep, and get fat.

But General Pope was rapidly concentrating his forces upon Manassas, intending, as he said, to "bag the whole bunch" of us, and General Jackson was too wary to stay there and get "bagged." Giving us time to eat our fill and provide ourselves with rations for at least three days, and ordering the destruction of the quantities of stores which lack of transportation made it impossible to take away, he that night moved his corps back towards Bull Run Mountain. Next day (August 28) he took a position from one to two miles beyond the turnpike running from Warrenton to Alexandria, with his left near where it crossed Bull Run and his right near Gainesville— a position favorable to either awaiting the arrival of General Longstreet's corps or falling back upon it in case of being hard pressed and compelled to retreat.

General Jackson did not, like the overconfident General Pope, deem lines of retreat unworthy of consideration. He deemed it wise to take every possible precaution against unexpected contingencies; and knowing how a very small thing—a slight misunderstanding of orders by one officer, a little delay by another, or any one of many unforeseen happenings—may cause the plans of the ablest commander to miscarry and turn the tide of battle against him, he, like every general worthy of the rank, always endeavored to prudently keep open a line of retreat. He did not shrink from taking chances when circumstances demanded it, and was often daring in his movements; but he was never foolhardy. I have heard that, on one occasion, a certain Colonel asked for permission to take his regiment on an expedition into the zone of danger for the purpose of capturing what was reported to be a small force of the enemy holding an isolated position.

"If your attempt should fail, how would you get your regiment back?" asked the General.

"I've not considered such a possibility," was the reply.

"It is well to consider possibilities and consequences, Colonel," said Jackson; "and, if you can't see how you could get your regiment out in case of failure, perhaps you'd better not take it in."

General Pope, having failed to "bag" us at Manassas, pushed forward to attack us before the rest of General Lee's army could be brought up to our aid. Soon after the formation of our line of battle along the Warrenton turnpike was completed, the Federals appeared. A strong column of them was seen, bearing down upon the division of General Taliaferro, which was on our right. A rapid and effective fire from our batteries caused them to halt. Our division was then ordered to Taliaferro's support, and favorably placed to oppose any farther advance they might make. For awhile, with the exception of a slow artillery duel, things were quiet. They were making their arrangements and waiting for reinforcements. About the middle of the afternoon, they moved forward and attacked us with determination and vigor. When one line was driven back, another pressed forward. We repelled attack after attack. The battle raged fiercely

The Battle of Second Manassas (Bull Run)
(August 29–30, 1862)
Jackson's men destroying Union supplies at Manassas

J. W. Bitley Funeral Homes, Richmond, Va.

until nightfall, when the enemy retired. The loss on both sides was heavy. General Ewell, our division commander, lost a leg; and many men of his division failed to answer at the next roll-call.

To be ready for a possible night attack, we slept where we were when the fight ended, with our guns beside us; but our slumber was not disturbed.

Before going to sleep, I found it necessary to satisfy the demands of my inner man, which, having been neglected since early morning, became quite insistent as the excitement of battle died down. Reaching into my haversack, I drew out a piece of fat pickled pork and some hardtack—the rations I had selected from the varied assortment at Manassas. Scraping the raw pork with a knife and spreading the scrapings on the hardtack, as one butters bread, I made one of the most delicious and satisfying meals I ever ate. I can bear witness that a keen appetite can make raw pork and hardtack exceedingly palatable.

On the following morning, no enemy appeared in our immediate front, and our brigade was sent to protect the right flank of Jackson's position. Too few to form a line of battle long enough to cover the front to be protected, we were deployed as skirmishers, our line extending across the Warrenton turnpike. We remained there until relieved by the arrival of General Longstreet's troops, but nothing occurred more important than an occasional exchange of shots with the enemy's outlying pickets.

We were then hurried to the left to support Hill's division, which, assailed by greatly superior numbers, had been fiercely engaged for some time and was being sorely pressed. When we reached the scene of conflict, there was a lull in the fighting, Hill's brigades having been forced to withdraw because their ammunition was exhausted. Our brigade was formed in line of battle along the edge of a field about half a mile wide, with woods on the farther side. About twenty yards back in these woods, was the unused railroad cut to which this battle gave a place in history. For its possession both sides had been fighting, and I was told it had been taken and retaken several times as the contending forces were borne back and forth. It was then held by the Federals, and the work cut out for us was to drive them out.

It would have been a waste of powder and ball to shoot at an enemy lurking in a railroad cut which the woods concealed from view, and we were wisely ordered to double-quick forward, trailing our guns and reserving our fire. As we pressed on, I heard the zip of a few bullets, but they came from skirmishers. The main line was waiting for us to come in close range. Just as we were entering the woods, the waiting Federals greeted us with a volley. Luckily, they aimed too high, and most of their balls went over our heads. Before they could reload, we were upon them; and all, except a few dozen who failed to scramble out of the cut quick enough to avoid capture, fled into the woods beyond.

The fighting blood of our men was up; and, instead of stopping in the cut, they hurried on in pursuit of the fleeing foe. They heard cannon booming off to their left; and, yelling: "Let's take that battery," started in the direction of the sound. Officers, realizing the folly and danger of such a mad rush ran out in front of their companies and tried to halt them. That I had read about cowboys trying to head off a stampeded herd came into my mind. I saw General Early riding down the line, swearing at the men, and ordering them to halt. When he came near me, I looked up into his flushed and perspiring face and laughingly asked: "Aren't you going to let them take that battery, General?" "Take hell! Go back to that railroad cut, and take all the other damn fools you can get to go with you," was his answer. (His best friends will say that he <u>sometimes</u> used profane language.)

Soon, the battle-lust of the men was cooled down, and they went quietly back to the railroad cut. A little after sunrise next morning, when we were sitting in the cut, a sharpshooter, firing from a tree away off on our left, wounded me and two other men and killed the second lieutenant of our company. The Federal sharpshooters had long-range rifles, with telescope-sights. My wound, although not very serious, sent me to the hospital.

A very large man, Jim Ferris of the 5th Texas found himself in a dilapidated state of dress as Second Manassas ended. His pants were too short and his ankles were lacerated and bleeding. Deciding that the estate of a dead Yankee might provide him a pair of leggings, he roamed over the field of the dead, searching for a corpse of appropriate size and wondering if there really were ghosts. Finding a body of suitable size, he began to remove the leggings. Suddenly the "corpse" sat up and exclaimed, "Great God alive, man! Don't rob me before I'm dead, if you please!" The horrified Ferris sprang about 20 feet at one bound before recovering himself and apologizing. He gave the wounded man his canteen before leaving. Rather than risk waking another "corpse" he decided to do without leggings and just return to his camp. On the way he came across another large man lying full length on the ground and wearing leggings. Ferris put his hand on the man's shoulder, gave it a shake, and asked, "Say, mister, are you dead or alive?" Receiving no response Ferris was soon the proud possessor of a magnificent pair of linen leggings.

CHAPTER VI

Battle of Chancellorsville

The winter of 1862–63 passed quietly, the two armies facing each other from opposite sides of the Rappahannock River. Our rude huts were dry and warm, and we were fairly comfortable in spite of wintry weather. There was little drilling, the old-timers being deemed proficient enough and the newcomers, who were not many, being drilled in squads.

The monotony of camp-life was relieved in various ways. In bad weather, the men stayed in their narrow quarters and whiled away the hours chatting, reading novels, and playing indoor games. When the weather was favorable, there were wrestling matches, foot-races, ball-games, and other outdoor sports.

During several weeks of the winter, the ground was covered with snow; and then opposing armies were formed and pitched battles fought, with snowballs as the ammunition. These battles were not fought in a haphazard and disorderly way; but each army was duly officered, and all its movements were directed by a commander. Under his direction and supervision, the best available position was selected and fortified beforehand, and an abundant supply of ammunition was prepared and placed along the line within easy reach of the men. And when the fight was on, he watched its progress, and maneuvered his troops for advantageous attack or defense. Some of these battles were won by tactics that would not have discredited a military leader of renown. At times the fighting, as in modern football, was rather rough; but, on the whole, it was fine sport. Of course, no one was killed in these engagements; but the slightly wounded and the captured were many. Prisoners were paroled as soon as taken; and, by the rules of the game, all the wounded were supposed to be hors de combat and compelled to withdraw from the fight.

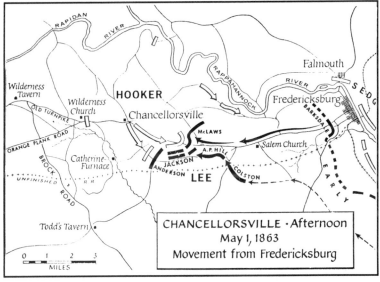

Clifford Dowdey

As winter passed and spring approached, we noticed a good deal of activity among the Federals, who were then commanded by General Hooker. Alluding to this activity, General Lee, in a letter since published, said: "General Hooker is obliged to do something: I do not know what it will be. He is playing the Chinese game, trying what frightening will do. He runs out his guns, starts his wagons and troops up and down the river, and creates an excitement generally. Our men look on in wonder, give a cheer, and all again subsides in statu quo ante bellum." But "Marse Robert" could be neither frightened nor deceived by such maneuvering. He quietly watched, and awaited developments.

Near the end of April, when it was evident that the enemy was about to begin operations in earnest, and intended to cross the Rappahannock either near the town of Fredericksburg or at some of the fords above, our corps was withdrawn from its city of huts down the river, and went into camp on the edge of the woods along the railroad between Fredericksburg and Hamilton's Crossing. The men said it was almost the same position they had held when they hurled back the attacking Federals on the 13th of December. Behind us was a low wooded hill. In our front, a plain, more than a mile in width, stretched away to the river. Through this plain, almost parallel with the railroad and about half way between it and the river, ran a public road. Along the sides of this highway, were embankments, two or three feet high, on which fences had once stood. We had pickets posted in the shelter of these embankments.

On the 28th of April, the Federals—General Sedgwick's corps, 30,000 strong—appeared on the Stafford Heights just below Fredericksburg; and next morning they crossed the river and took up a position in our front. "'Looks like we're goin' to fight the battle of Fredericksburg over again," said one of our men.

"Here we are, just as we were then; and there are the Yankees, just as they were then; and it looks like they're gettin' ready to attack us, just as they did then." "Don't let looks fool you, old boy," said another. "If 'Fighting Joe' Hooker, as they call him, isn't an ass, he won't adopt Burnside's tactics. I don't know what he's going to do; but it's a safe bet that this demonstration in our front is only a feint, and that his main attack will be made somewhere else."

This proved to be the case. Having got his corps into position on our side of the river, General Sedgwick assumed a waiting attitude. During the rest of that day and throughout the next, no move was made by either side in our locality. On the morning of May 1st, we heard (what our commander had probably heard before) that General Hooker, with the main part of his army, had crossed the river at the upper fords, and was moving against the Confederate left and rear by way of Chancellorsville, some ten or twelve miles west

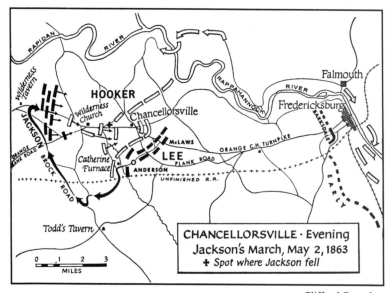

CHANCELLORSVILLE · Evening
Jackson's March, May 2, 1863
✚ Spot where Jackson fell

Clifford Dowdey

of Fredericksburg. Leaving General Early, with his own division, a brigade of Mississippians, and a detachment of artillery, to hold Sedgwick in check, General Lee moved in the direction of Chancellorsville with the rest of his army to arrest the advance of General Hooker.

Knowing that his small force could not long hold its ground against a determined attack by General Sedgwick's 30,000, General Early skilfully maneuvered his troops so as to make a show of great strength and deter the enemy from making an attack. From the demonstrations in his front, General Sedgwick probably thought that the whole Confederate army was directly before him, and was confidently expecting Hooker's advance to force it out of its position and give him a chance to effectively strike its retreating divisions. Whatever his reason may have been, he remained inactive for more than two days, when a forward movement by him would probably have saved his chief from disaster.

On the evening of the 2nd of May, after building many camp-fires to make the enemy think we were still there, we were withdrawn from our position, and started on a night march to join General Lee. When we had made about half the distance, the order was countermanded, and we returned to front Sedgwick. Reaching his front a little after sunrise next morning, we found things as we had left them, except that the enemy's outposts had been moved forward. This was discovered when my regiment, deployed as skirmishers, advanced to occupy the road our pickets had held. Before we reached it, the Federals began firing upon us from the shelter of its embankments. At once, we saw that we must either fall back ourselves or drive them back. Our Colonel decided to do the latter, and ordered us to "charge." We dashed forward at full speed. The Federals greeted us with a volley which, as we were in open formation, did little damage; and then, realizing that we would be upon them before they could reload, took to their heels.

As we neared the road, a battery posted in the field beyond, and until then hid from our view, opened on us with grapeshot. Luckily, the gunners had to aim a little high to clear the embankments, and most of their charges went over us, making a whirring and fluttering sound like that made by a flock of quail when rising from cover. They, however, killed several of our men and wounded others before we reached shelter. Then, safely ensconced behind the embankments, we evened up matters by sending the artillerymen musket balls in return for the grapeshot they had sent us. When a number of them had fallen and they saw that they were completely at our mercy, they quickly limbered up and hurried away, taking their killed and wounded with them.

In connection with this little affair, I recall an incident that was both amusing and pathetic. In our regiment, was a young fellow who had joined us while we were in winter quarters and was that morning having his first experience of how it feels to be under fire. He conducted himself as bravely as the bravest as long as only musket balls were zipping past him; but, when the artillery opened on us and he heard the whur-r-t, whur-r-t of grapeshot hurtling through the air near his head, he lost his nerve. We didn't run back; neither did he, like the rest of us, make a fresh spurt for the shelter of the embankment some twenty yards ahead of us. He fell prone on the ground, and, as fast as he could give utterance to the cry, screamed "Lord-av-mercy, Lord-av-mercy." He continued to lie there and scream for mercy until we had driven the battery away and he could no longer hear the nerve-shaking sound of the grapeshot.

A few minutes after the battery was driven from our front, I saw it, or another like it, wheeling into position on a slight elevation nearly a mile off to our left. The Federals were evidently getting ready to enfilade us; and, seeing that our Colonel was looking through his field-glasses at the movements of the enemy in front and had not noticed this menace to our flank, I called his attention to it. Walking out into the road to get a better view and make his own observations, he asked: "Where is the battery?" As I raised my hand to point it out, there was a puff of smoke; and, an instant later, a shell exploded almost directly over our heads. A large fragment of it struck the ground about five feet before us and besprinkled us with the dirt of the road. "I see it, I see it," exclaimed the Colonel; and, turning to me, he ordered: "Run to the General, and tell him, with my compliments, that it will be impossible to hold this position unless that battery can be silenced." I hurried away to our Brigadier, who was back on the railroad with the rest of his command; but, before I reached him, the commander of our artillery, sizing up the situation, opened on the battery and quickly silenced it.

When, well-nigh exhausted from running, I drew near to the General, he waved his hand in greeting, and shouted: "Hurrah for the gallant 13th." That we had displayed unusual gallantry had not occurred to me. As I saw it, we had merely run forward, facing the enemy's fire, because that was the shortest way to shelter and the safest thing to do. But the General seemed to think we had done something uncommonly courageous. When I delivered the Colonel's message, he said: "Tell your Colonel his wishes were anticipated. Present my compliments and hearty congratulations to him and the brave men of his splendid regiment. I watched their brilliant and victorious charge with profound admiration, and I feel that it is truly a great honor to be in command of such men." The General had been a famous stump speaker in the peaceful days of the country, and war had not cured him of the habit.

While such byplays were being enacted in the vicinity of Fredericksburg, momentous events were taking place in the vicinity of Chancellorsville. On the 1st of May, the Confederates met the advance of General Hooker's army, and drove it back on the main body. On the 2nd, the Federals being so strongly intrenched that it was deemed inadvisable to attack their front, Jackson made his famous flank movement, and, swooping down upon their surprised right, threw it into confusion and swept everything before him until night ended the conflict. On the morning of the 3rd, the victorious Confederates resumed the battle with unabated vigor; and, although their lines had been reformed during the night and they made a stubborn resistance, the Federals were driven from one after another of their positions and the destruction of the Army of the Potomac seemed imminent.

Then General Sedgwick set out to aid his sorely pressed chief. A little before noon of the 3rd, he broke through the left of our thin line and took the road to Chancellorsville; but, before getting far on his way, he was halted and held in check overnight by troops withdrawn from General Hooker's front. Next morning, General Early moved in between him and Fredericksburg, so that both his front and rear were threatened. We remained quietly in that position until we were ready to attack, although he could have extricated himself from it by overwhelming Early's comparatively small force and returning to Fredericksburg.

General Lee's plan was to attack him from both sides at the same time; and it was arranged that Early should advance to the attack at a given signal announcing the readiness of the troops on the Chancellorsville side. We waited for four or five hours with nothing more exciting than an occasional exchange of shots along the skirmish lines. Then, when the sun was low in the west, we heard the boom—boom—boom of three distinct cannon shots. It was the appointed signal; and the men, at the order to "fall in," sprang to their places in the ranks with arms shouldered. "Forward, double-quick march"; and, promptly obeying the command, the line moved with rapid strides towards the hill on which the Federals were posted. As it approached the base of the hill, a storm of deadly missiles burst upon it; but steadily, unwaveringly it moved forward. Then the officers shouted "Charge"; and the men, breaking into a run and wildly cheering, swept on up the slope. Before their impetuous charge, the enemy broke and fled. In less than fifteen minutes after the signal shots were fired, the Federals were

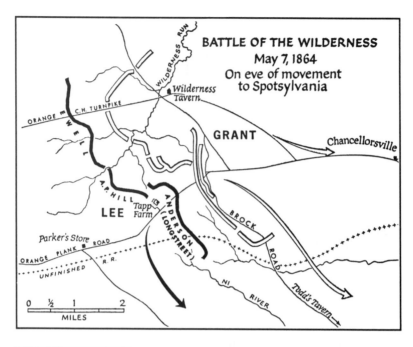

BATTLE OF THE WILDERNESS
May 7, 1864
On eve of movement
to Spotsylvania

WILDERNESS RUN

ORANGE C.H. TURNPIKE

W E L L

Wilderness
Tavern

GRANT

Chancellorsville

A.P. HILL

LEE
Tapp
Farm

A N D E R S O N
(LONGSTREET)

BROCK

ROAD

Parker's Store

ORANGE PLANK ROAD
R. R.
UNFINISHED

NI

RIVER

Todd's Tavern

0   ½   1   2
MILES

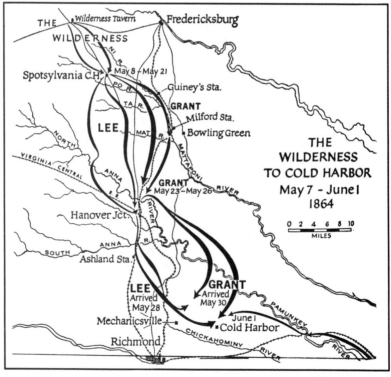

THE
WILDERNESS

Wilderness Tavern

Fredericksburg

NI

Spotsylvania C.H.
PO R.
May 8 – May 21

Guiney's Sta.

TA R.

GRANT

Milford Sta.

LEE
MAT R.

Bowling Green

NORTH

ANNA

VIRGINIA CENTRAL

R. R.

GRANT
May 23–May 26

MATTAPONI

RIVER

THE
WILDERNESS
TO COLD HARBOR
May 7 - June 1
1864

0   2   4   6   8 10
MILES

Hanover Jct.

ANNA

R.

SOUTH

Ashland Sta.

RIVER

LEE
Arrived
May 28

GRANT
Arrived
May 30

PAMUNKEY

Mechanicsville

June 1
Cold Harbor

Richmond

CHICKAHOMINY

RIVER

RIVER

Clifford Dowdey

in full retreat with our men in hot pursuit. The attack from the direction of Chancellorsville was equally successful, and, but for the coming of night to end the pursuit, Sedgwick's corps would have been destroyed. Under cover of the darkness, it "stole away" to one of the upper fords of the Rappahannock and found safety on the other side of the river.

Although General Sedgwick's advance proved so disastrous to his own corps, it was the salvation of General Hooker's army. To meet it, General Lee was compelled to withdraw troops from Hooker's front; and that officer, wisely taking advantage of the respite thus given him, hurried his army to safety as rapidly as possible. When General Lee returned to the field of Chancellorsville to finish him, it was found that he, too, had "stolen away."

Thus the battle of Chancellorsville ended in a complete victory for the Confederates, notwithstanding the fact that, in all save generalship and valor, the odds were heavily against them. General Hooker's army was about three times as strong as General Lee's numerically; and it was so advantageously placed that, with ordinarily skilful handling, its success seemed certain.

It is said that, on reaching Chancellorsville, General Hooker boasted: "The Confederate army is now the legitimate property of the Army of the Potomac"; and, had his action been as confident and bold as his speech, it is more than probable he would have made good his boast. This must be evident to any one who considers the relative positions of the opposing armies. On the morning of the 1st of May, Sedgwick with 30,000 men was at Fredericksburg, Hooker with 90,000 men was at Chancellorsville, and the Confederate army was almost directly between them. Had both Hooker and Sedgwick pressed boldly forward that day, attacking from Fredericksburg and Chancellorsville at the same time, General Lee would have been unable to successfully withdraw the greater part of his army from Sedgwick's front to oppose Hooker, would have been given no time for the flank movement by which he won the battle, and would have been forced to retreat to save his army from destruction. But, instead of boldly advancing, Sedgwick's 30,000, with only 9,000 to oppose them, remained at Fredericksburg until the 3rd, without so much as feeling the strength of the line in their front; and Hooker's 90,000, with only 12,000 to oppose them, kept behind their breastworks at Chancellorsville throughout the 2nd, giving Jackson time to reach their flank by a long detour and fall upon it like a bolt from a clear sky. By the timidity and tardiness of his tactics, the Federal Commander enabled his more skilful adversary to wrest from him the victory that was within his reach.

Among those who fought their last battle at Chancellorsville was General T. J. "Stonewall" Jackson, who, after night had closed the conflict on the 2nd, rode out in front of his lines with some members of his staff to observe the position of the enemy, and was wounded by his own men, who mistook the party for Federals. His wounds were not in themselves mortal, but complications arose and he died on the 10th of May. His brilliant achievements had crowned him with imperishable fame and ranked him with the world's greatest soldiers. His loss was irreparable, and some think it changed the result of the war.

At a Confederate Reunion in Richmond, I chanced to overhear a conversation between two veterans who were looking at the Jackson monument that stands in the Capitol Square of that city. "God killed him," said one. "He didn't want the South to win; and, seeing she'd win if Jackson lived, He aimed the bullet that killed him." "Then," replied the other, "God isn't as good a marksman as I thought He was. I've always thought that, if God were to aim a bullet to kill a man, He'd send it straight to some vital spot, instead of bungling the job by wounding an arm and a hand and having to get up a lot of complications to make the wounds fatal." Expressed less bluntly, I have often heard the opinion stated by the first of these speakers—the opinion that the South would have won had Jackson lived, and that his death was brought about by a direct interposition of Divine Providence to prevent such a result. Apart from the fact that this notion carries with it a reflection on the methods of Divine Providence, I think there lies against it the fact that Jackson's death was not necessary to defeat the South.

The South was not defeated because she lacked generals, but because she lacked men. Every battle she fought—every victory she won—robbed her ranks of men whom she could not replace; and, as this process of attrition went on, her lines finally became so thin and weak that they could not possibly withstand the overwhelming numbers of the constantly repleted armies of the North. Had the men lost by General Lee in the victories he won been with him to strengthen his weak lines in front of Petersburg, I believe he would have defeated Grant without the aid of Jackson; and, had Jackson been with him without the men, the battle-flags of the Army of Northern Virginia would have been furled in defeat just the same.

It is true that Jackson was General Lee's "right arm"—his ablest executive officer; but it is not true, as some seem to think, that he originated the strategic movements by which General Lee's victories were won. He did not, as some of his biographers claim, conceive and suggest the flank movement which defeated Hooker. The truth is that, when asked how to get at the enemy, he made no suggestion whatever, and General Lee alone devised the plan. Major Talcott, of General Lee's staff, in a letter telling of the last interview between Lee and Jackson, extracts from which are given in General Long's "memoirs," says: "At this time," (about ten o'clock on the night of May 1st) "Generals Lee and Jackson were together, and Lee, who had a map before him, asked Jackson: 'How can we get at these people?' To which Jackson replied, in effect; 'You know best. Show me what to do, and we will try to do it.' General Lee looked thoughtfully at the map; then indicated on it and explained the movement he desired General Jackson to make." Honor to whom honor is due. To Lee belongs the honor of planning that famous movement; to Jackson belongs the honor of brilliantly executing it.

CHAPTER VII

Battle of Gettysburg

When the Army of Northern Virginia invaded Pennsylvania, I was left, with my regiment; on duty in Winchester, and remained there until it returned. I stood in front of the provost marshal's office and saw the men as they wearily marched through the town on their way southward. They plainly showed the grievous effects of "stress and strain." The long, toilsome marches, the desperate fighting, and the manifold hardships of the campaign had told upon them heavily. They were more ragged and unkempt, more worn and haggard, more slow in their movements, and more grave and silent than I had ever before seen them. They did not seem beaten and cowed; they seemed rather to be conscious of adverse fortune and grimly determined to face it bravely. But they looked dog-tired; and, as some one standing near me said, they seemed to be ashamed of coming back to their friends without having accomplished all that was hoped for.

But those toil-worn and battle-scarred men who came back from Gettysburg had no cause for shame. If they had failed to accomplish all it was hoped they would, the fault was not theirs. Bravely and nobly they had done their part. If they had not won victory, they had won imperishable glory. When the battle of Gettysburg is mentioned, the thought which first comes to the mind, and remains most prominent, is not of the blue-coated host on the crest of Cemetery Ridge, but of the gray-clad heroes who dauntlessly charged up its slope in the face of a deadly storm of shot and shell. Every artist who endeavors to represent that battle on canvas gives to those gray-clad heroes the foremost place in the picture. President Lincoln, as reported, when shown the position defended by the soldiers of the North and assailed by the soldiers of the South, said: "I am proud to be the countryman of the men who assailed those heights," and thus indirectly recognized the preeminent display of courage made by the assailants. The Federals claimed victory, but the Confederates brought off the honors of the field. Describing the charge of Pickett's Virginians, an English historian says: "The charge of the Light Brigade was less desperate and its trial far less prolonged. The bravest among the victors of Inkerman or Albuera, of Worth and Gravelotte, might envy the glory of Pickett's defeat."

And why did the dauntless courage and heroic efforts of the Confederates fail to win victory at Gettysburg? This question, which has called forth much discussion since, was asked by the men of the army at the time, and they freely expressed the belief that "some one had blunder'd." A few of those with whom I talked, while still reposing confidence in their greatly loved commander, attributed the blunder to him; and it is worthy of note that they thought his supposed mistake resulted from overestimating the prowess and efficiency of his soldiers. A young officer said to me: "I think General Lee was dazzled by contemplating the splendid results that would ensue from victory. He saw Philadelphia, Baltimore, and Washington at his mercy, and the independence of the Confederacy almost certainly won; and the vision blinded him to the fact that his men could not accomplish the impossible, and led him to make the fatal mistake of sending them against an impregnable position." Had that young officer known all the facts since brought to light, I think he would have held a very different opinion. These facts, stated by men of unquestionable veracity who relate what they themselves saw and heard, show that, instead of being "dazzled" and "blinded," General Lee was calm and clear-sighted, fully appreciated the difficulties that confronted him, sent his men against nothing more formidable than what they had successfully encountered on other fields, and skilfully laid plans that would have resulted in complete victory if they had been faithfully carried out.

Just after the repulse of Pickett's column, when that officer was sobbingly lamenting the frightful loss sustained by his division, General Lee, it is reported, soothingly said to him: "Never mind, General—all this has been my fault"; but it does not follow that the fault was really his. He may have been moved to take the blame upon himself, not only by a generous impulse to save his gallant subordinate from any feeling of self-reproach, but also by the desire to prevent him from reproaching others and thereby creating bad blood and dissensions. Later, when General Pickett made a report of the famous charge and somewhat severely reflected upon others, General Lee returned it to him with a letter saying: "You and your men have crowned yourselves with glory; but we have the enemy to fight, and must carefully, at this critical moment, guard against dissensions which the reflections in your report will create. I will therefore suggest that you destroy both copy and original, substituting one confined to casualties merely." It is easy to understand how the strong desire to "guard against dissensions" that led him to request the suppression of the facts set forth in Pickett's report may have led him to magnanimously assume blame when he was blameless.

The Confederate failure at Gettysburg was not due to any mistake made by General Lee, but to the disregard of his orders by his subordinates. Through the failure of subordinates to follow his instructions and carry out his plans, it came to pass that the battle of Gettysburg was fought neither <u>where</u> nor <u>as</u> he intended.

Before General Lee left Fredericksburg to invade Pennsylvania, as a member of his staff testifies, he anticipated being forced to give battle in the vicinity of either Chambersburg, York, or Gettysburg; and he preferred the last named place, as nearer his base and affording better facilities for keeping his line of communication open. But he expected to select his own battle-ground and have his army in an advantageous position. his expectation was defeated because, contrary to his instructions, his cavalry—"the eyes and ears of the army"—had been led out of communication with him, leaving him without information as to the enemy's movements and, to a large extent, compelled to "feel his way in the dark." General Long, in his Memoirs, says: "Previous to the passage of the Potomac, General Stuart was instructed to make the movements of his cavalry correspond with those of the Federal army, so that he might be in position to observe and report all important information. . . . But on this occasion, either from the misapprehension of instructions or the love of the eclat of a bold raid, Stuart, instead of maintaining his appropriate position between the armies, placed himself on the right flank of the enemy, where his communication with Lee was effectually severed. This greatly embarrassed the movements of General Lee, and eventually forced him to an engagement under disadvantageous circumstances."

Had General Stuart followed the instructions given him, kept the cavalry where it properly belonged, and promptly reported the enemy's advance, General Lee would have had ample time to concentrate his army at Gettysburg, and place it in the most advantageous position for the battle, before the Federals arrived. As it was, he did not learn that they had crossed the Potomac and reached Frederick until the night of June 28th, when the news was brought by an infantry scout. He immediately ordered the junction of his corps at Gettysburg, but it was then too late to reach that place ahead of the Federals.

The first Confederate troops that reached the vicinity—Heth's division of Hill's corps—encountered Federal cavalry three or four miles out from the town, and, driving it in, found it supported by two army corps under the command of General Reynolds. Bringing up Pender's division to aid Heth's, General Hill attacked this force with his usual impetuosity, and, assisted by two of Ewell's divisions that arrived just in time, totally defeated it and drove it from the field in disorderly flight. But the advantage gained was not immediately followed up.

Lacking information as to the location of the Federal troops, naturally supposing them to be in strong force on or near the ridge to which the defeated corps had retreated, and deeming it imprudent to risk bringing on a general engagement with only four or five divisions of the army up, the officers present halted the pursuit. Had they known, as the cavalry ought to have been in its place to inform them, that the main body of the Federal army was still miles away, they could and would have taken Cemetery Ridge that afternoon. General Rodes, who commanded one of Ewell's divisions in the engagement, afterwards said in my hearing: "I was halted when I could have carried the heights without losing fifty more men."

In his "Lost Cause," Mr. E. A. Pollard charges General Lee with the failure to follow up the victory of the first day. He says: "As Ewell and Hill prepared for a fresh attack, they were halted by General Lee, who deemed it advisable to abstain from pressing his advantage until the arrival of the remainder of his army." But Mr. Pollard was far from the scene of conflict, and his statement is hardly consistent with that of Colonel Walter R. Taylor, who was on the ground and, as Lee's adjutant-general, in a position to know the facts. General Lee did not reach the field until near the close of the first day's battle; and, in Southern Historical Society Papers, Colonel Taylor says: "Later, General Lee rode over to General Ewell's front and conferred as to future movements. He wanted to follow up the success gained—thought that with Johnson's division, then up, General Ewell could go forward at dawn next day. Ewell, Early, and Rodes thought it best to await Longstreet's arrival and make the main attack on the enemy's left. This was determined on." Longstreet with two of his divisions was then only four miles off, and the ground before the enemy's left was much more favorable for attack than that in Ewell's front.

A reconnaissance of the Federal position on Cemetery Ridge revealed the fact that, although fresh troops had arrived and the ridge was held by a considerable force, a large part of Meade's army had not come up. On hearing this, General Lee at once determined to attack at an early hour next morning, before the arrival of the whole Federal force, and before the part of it already up could make thorough preparation for resistance. The time fixed for the attack was sunrise. At that hour, as ordered, Ewell was to assail Meade's right, Longstreet was to assail his left, and Hill was to hold his corps in position to give assistance where it might be needed. All of Longstreet's corps had not arrived; but, as he admits in his report, he received orders to move with the portion of his command that was then up."

An idea of the situation at sunrise next morning—the time fixed for the attack—may be gathered from a statement made by General W. N. Pendleton, chief of artillery, in an address delivered at Lexington, Virginia, in 1873. He says: "The ground southwest of the town was carefully examined by me after the engagement on July 1st. Being found much less difficult than the steep ascent fronting the troops already up, its practicable character was reported to our commanding General. He informed me that he had ordered Longstreet to attack on that front at sunrise the next morning. And he added to myself, 'I want you to be out long before sunrise so as to reexamine and save time.' He also desired me to communicate with General Longstreet as well as with himself. The reconnaissance was accordingly made, as soon as it was light enough on the 2nd, and made through a long distance—in fact, very close to what there was of the enemy's line. No insuperable difficulty appearing, and marching up— far off—the enemy's reenforcing columns being seen, the extreme desirableness of immediate attack there was at once reported to the commanding General; and, according to his wish, message was also sent to the intrepid but deliberate corps commander whose sunrise attack there had been ordered."

This statement effectually disposes of the assertion that, "on the night of the 1st of July, General Meade . . . concentrated his entire army on those critical heights of Gettysburg," and refutes the opinion that General Lee blundered in ordering an attack next morning. General Pendleton, before sunrise on the morning of the 2nd, made a thorough reconnaissance "through a long distance," "very close to what there was of the enemy's line," and saw "far off, the enemy's reenforcing columns" marching up. The Federals were not on the ridge in full force. In fact, the Peach Orchard and Little Round Top, that later in the day became the scenes of fierce and bloody conflict, had not then been occupied by the Federals, and could have been taken by the Confederates without firing a gun. There

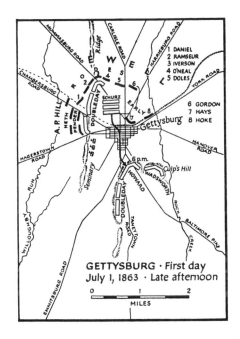

GETTYSBURG · First day
July 1, 1863 · Late afternoon

0   1   2
MILES

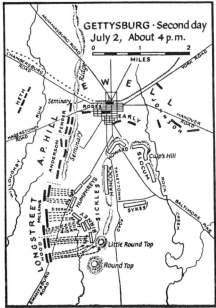

GETTYSBURG · Second day
July 2, About 4 p.m.

0   1   2
MILES

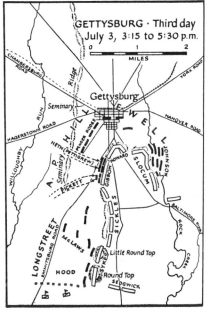

GETTYSBURG · Third day
July 3, 3:15 to 5:30 p.m.

0   1   2
MILES

Clifford Dowdey

was "no insuperable difficulty"—nothing to prevent a completely successful attack.

But the early morning attack that General Lee ordered was not made because General Longstreet assumed the responsibility of delaying it. At sunrise, his divisions, that bivouacked for the night within four miles of the battle-field, were not in position to attack. The sun mounted high in the heavens, and still they did not arrive. While the enemy's reinforcing columns could be seen afar off; while "the advantage in numbers and readiness which the Confederate army possessed was rapidly disappearing"; and while General Lee was becoming more and more impatient and uneasy, and wondering what could be detaining Longstreet, that officer, coolly disregarding the order of his commanding General to "move with that portion of his command which was up," was waiting for the arrival of another brigade, because, as he said, he feared that his force then up was "too weak to venture to make an attack."

Instead of attacking in the early morning as ordered, Longstreet did not attack until after 4 o'clock in the afternoon, when the entire Army of the Potomac was in position and the hope of defeating the enemy in detail was gone. Had he moved as ordered, "with that portion of his command which was up," he could have occupied without opposition the ground from which he succeeded in driving the Federals after a severe and costly struggle, and Little Round Top from which he failed to drive them; and holding Little Round Top, "the key-point of that whole section of the battlefield," he could have taken the Federal line in reverse and made victory certain. As it was, his troops, after a long conflict in which their loss was heavy, forced the enemy back and reached the base of Cemetery Ridge; but they were too nearly exhausted to carry the heights, crowned with infantry behind breastworks and bristling with artillery.

A combined drive against the Federal right and left early on the morning of the 2nd, when only a part of General Meade's army was up and two of the corps that were up had been beaten with heavy loss and greatly disorganized the day before, could not have failed. On the morning of the 3rd, such a drive, though less certain of success, seemed likely to succeed. At this point in his account of the battle, General Long says: "Though Cemetery Ridge remained intact in the hands of the Federals, yet the engagement had resulted at every point in an advantage to the Confederates. Longstreet had cleared his front of the enemy, and occupied the ground from which they had been driven. Ewell's left held the breastworks on Culp's Hill on the extreme right of the Federal line. Meade's army was known to have sustained heavy losses. There was, in consequence, good reason to believe that a renewed assault might prove successful. . . . General Lee therefore determined to renew the assault."

Ewell and Longstreet, the latter being reinforced for the purpose, were directed to move simultaneously early on the morning of the 3rd—the one against the enemy's right and the other against his left. Ewell attacked promptly; but Longstreet was not ready to move at the same time, and Ewell's men, after courageously battling for four hours, were compelled to yield the breastworks they had captured, and retire before the greatly superior force thrown against them.

In view of the changed conditions thus brought about, General Lee abandoned the plan of simultaneously assailing the enemy's wings, and decided on the attempt to pierce the Federal line at a comparatively weak point near its center, assail its right in flank, and, with the aid of Ewell and Hill—the former assailing its other flank and the latter threatening its front—completely crush it. The task of piercing the line was assigned to Longstreet, as his corps was in front of the point to be assailed.

The plan of attack having been fully discussed and the necessary preparations having been made, the signal for battle was given. One hundred and forty-five guns that had been massed for the attack concentrated their fire on the Federal position. The Federal batteries quickly and vigorously responded. The reverberating thunder of the cannonade rent the air and shook the hills. One who was present writes: "For one hour and a half this most terrific fire was continued, during which time the shrieking of shell, the crash of falling timber, the fragments of rocks flying through the air, shattered from the cliffs by solid shot, the heavy mutterings from the valley between the opposing armies, the splash of bursting shrapnel, and the fierce neighing of wounded artillery horses made a picture terribly grand and sublime."

Then came the great and tragic event with which the battle closed—Pickett's world-famous charge—the charge that won for him and his gallant Virginians a place in the roll of fame along with the most illustrious of those whose feats of marvellous valor illumine the pages of history.

When the terrific cannonade ceased, the troops that were to make the assault—Pickett's division, Heth's division, and, according to the statement of General Long, Wilcox's brigade—came over the crest of the ridge behind which they had been lying, and, with the coolness, steadiness, and precision of a field-day parade, moved down the slope towards the narrow valley between the heights occupied by the two armies. Before them was a stretch of ground more than half a mile wide, every foot of which was in easy range of the enemy's guns; and the men knew that desperate work was ahead of them—that they were going where the air would be swarming with missiles of destruction, and death would reap a frightful harvest. But there was no halting, no faltering, no sign of weakening. With steady step and resolute courage the line moved forward. For a brief space, the Federals seemed to look on this splendid array with an admiration that amazed and silenced them; but, as the line advanced, their artillery opened upon it with a storm of death-dealing shot and shell, and, as it came nearer, their infantry poured upon it a still more deadly hail of bullets. The men of Heth's division—men of tried and proven valor who, in the first day's battle when their gallant division commander was wounded, had behaved with unsurpassed courage—were thrown into some disorder by the obstacles in their front, and, as a result of this confusion, recoiled before the terrific fire of the enemy. Seeing this, Wilcox, thinking the attack hopeless, halted his brigade, and the division of Pickett was left to go forward alone.

And forward that splendid division swept. Raising the "rebel yell" and breaking into a run, they dashed up the slope to the enemy's works with a courage that never faltered, although their ranks were torn and thinned by a fire such as few troops in the wars of the world have been called upon to face. "Steadily," says Pollard, "the Virginians press on. The name of Virginia was that day baptized in fire, and forever illuminated in the temple of history. There had been no such example of devotion in the war. Presently wild cries ring out; the smoke-masked troops are in the enemy's works; there is a hand-to-hand contest, and again and again the Confederate flag is lifted through the smoke over the shrinking columns of the enemy. Garnett is dead. Armistead is mortally wounded. Kemper is shot down. Every brigadier of the division is killed or wounded. But Pickett is unscathed in the storm; his flashing sword has taken the key of the enemy's position, and points the path of the conflict through his broken columns". . .

All honor to those brave Virginians. They behaved with a gallantry that has never been surpassed. Yet they only displayed, under circumstances that made it more conspicuous, a courage common to the Army of Northern Virginia. Behind them were men who, on other hotly contested fields, had proved themselves to be no less valorous, and who were ready to rush to the aid of their desperately battling comrade at the word of command. But the word of command was not given.

While Pickett's charge has thrilled the hearts of men with admiration, it has called forth much adverse criticism. It has been likened to the charge of the Light Brigade, which, although glorious, was a grievous blunder—a senseless sacrifice of heroic men. Writers have said: "It was magnificent, but it was not war"; and the world has criticized General Lee for sending that small force to dash itself to pieces against a strongly fortified position defended by overwhelming numbers. The answer to such criticism is: General Lee did not do it.

The plan of General Lee included adequate support of the assaulting column. General Longstreet was directed to support it with the other two divisions of his own corps—those of Hood and McLaws; and, if necessary, with troops from Hill's corps that were placed at his disposal for the purpose.

That Longstreet was so ordered is attested by officers in whose presence the order was given, and whose veracity is beyond question. General Lee's adjutant-general, Colonel Walter M. Taylor, in Southern Historical Society Papers, says: "Had Hood and McLaws followed or supported Pickett, and Pettigrew and Anderson been advanced, the design of the commanding General would have been carried out." General (then Colonel) A. L. Long, in his Memoirs, says: "The original intention of General Lee was that Pickett's attack should be supported by the divisions of McLaws and Hood, and General Longstreet was so ordered. This order was given verbally by General Lee in the presence of Colonel Long and Major Venable of his staff, and other officers of the army." Major Venable says: "I heard him" (General Lee) "give the orders when arranging the fight, and called his attention to it long afterward, when there was discussion about it. He said, 'I know it! I know it!' "

For some reason, the officer to whom this order was given failed to carry it out. "Hood and McLaws," says Colonel Taylor, were not moved forward . . . Anderson, who commanded one of Hill's divisions, made his dispositions to advance, but General Longstreet told him it was of no use—the attack had failed."

Would giving Pickett the support ordered have been "of no use"? What the men of Pickett's division did without support supplies an answer to the question. Says an eyewitness: "As they approached the ridge, their lines were torn by incessant volleys of musketry as by a deadly hail. Yet with unfaltering courage the brave fellows broke into the double-quick, and with an irresistible charge burst into the Federal lines and drove everything before them toward the crest of Cemetery Hill, leaping the breastworks and planting their standards on the captured guns with shouts of victory." They actually pierced the Federal line and, with overwhelming numbers closing in upon them from every side and a terrific fire concentrated upon them from every direction, they held the ground they had won for ten minutes. Had the no less courageous and resolute men of three other divisions been at hand to aid them, there is hardly room for doubt that the breach in Meade's line would have been maintained, and that his right, assailed in flank and rear on, that side and attacked by Ewell on the other, would have been completely defeated and probably destroyed. Instead of wondering why a charge so rash and seemingly hopeless was made, the world would be extolling the Napoleonic genius that planned and ordered it.

The reason for General Longstreet's failure to carry out his instructions can be only surmised. It is well known that he did not favor a frontal attack from the first. When consulted on the evening of the first day's battle, he suggested turning Meade's left as the best plan—a plan which General Lee, having no cavalry at hand to cover the movement and assist in collecting supplies for the army and realizing that such a movement would involve a dangerous extension of his lines in the presence of a superior force, deemed impracticable. Did General Longstreet, opposed to attacking the enemy's front, convinced that Pickett's assault would fail, and expecting that its failure would be followed by a Federal attack upon his own front, hold back the divisions of Hood, McLaws, and Anderson to repel the expected attack? This seems a wild conjecture; but it is suggested by the fact that he afterwards said: "I had Hood and McLaws, who had not been engaged; I had a heavy force of artillery; I should have liked nothing better than to have been attacked, and have no doubt that I should have given those who tried as bad a reception as Pickett received."

But whatever his reason for it may have been, I believe that his failure to obey the orders of his commanding General, first on the second day and again on the third day of the battle, deprived the Confederates of a complete and decisive victory—a victory which, as many have claimed, would have thoroughly disheartened the North and secured the independence of the Southern Confederacy.

From a political point of view, the battle of Gettysburg was unquestionably a great Federal victory, but, from the purely military view-point, it was a drawn battle. The Federal losses in the engagement—estimated by General Meade at 24,000 men killed, wounded, and missing—exceeded those of the Confederates by nearly 8,000. On the first and second days of the battle the Confederates were admittedly victorious; and on the third day, although Pickett's charge failed, Lee's army was not defeated. Even the men who had been repulsed were not disheartened. There was very little confusion. Colonel Freemantle, of the British army, who was present, says: "General Lee and his officers were fully impressed with a sense of the situation, yet there was much less noise, fuss, or confusion of orders than at an ordinary field-day. The men, as they were rallied in the wood, were brought up in detachments and lay down quietly and coolly in the positions assigned them." Their spirit was not broken, nor was their confidence in their commander shaken. "The army," says General Long, "was not discouraged or dispirited, and its sole wish was for an opportunity to efface the mortification of its first serious repulse."

But General Meade did not give it the opportunity. His army had sustained such heavy loss and had been thrown into such a state of confusion by the three days of battle that he was afraid to make an aggressive movement, although General Lee waited for him to do so during the rest of that day and throughout the next. In an article published in the *Atlantic Monthly*, General Howard said: "General Meade . . . realized fully the exact condition of affairs. Lee had been repulsed, not routed, and, if Meade had yielded to his own inclination to attack, he would have been repulsed himself, and would thus have thrown away the fruits of his great victory."

CHAPTER VIII

I Join the Signal Corps

When my regiment rejoined its brigade on the return of the army from Pennsylvania, I did not go with it. Much to my surprise, I was ordered to report for service in the Signal Corps. I had made no application for this service, and never certainly knew how I came to be selected for it. In the preceding summer, when we were encamped in Orange just before moving against General Pope, I had several times met the chief signal officer at the house of a kinsman, and I suppose he chanced to remember me when he needed another man.

Although the signal service was, for the most part, easier and less dangerous than that of a soldier in the ranks, I entered upon it with a good deal of reluctance. This was not because I loved hardships and dangers and regretted being, in some measure, free from them, but because I had come to love the brave and loyal men with whom I had so long shared the rigors and perils of an ordinary soldier's life, and was loath to leave them. I felt that I was breaking away from associates who had endeared themselves to me by many acts of unselfishness and kindness; parting from tried and true friends, many of whom I would probably never see again; sundering the ties of a brotherhood almost as close and tender as that of blood. Had I been free to act as my feelings prompted, I think I would have declined the new service and continued to fare with my old comrades.

The signal system, with which I was connected from that time until the close of the war, was the army's telegraph—an exceedingly crude means of conveying intelligence in comparison with the facilities possessed by the armies of the present day. Not having the modern inventions and appliances by means of which the commanding General is informed of all that is going on and the subordinate commanders are kept in close touch with him and with one another, messages were sent by signaling through stations located on mountains, hills, or other elevations. These stations were more or less distant from one another, according to the topography of the country and the power of the telescopes used in taking the messages; and the signals were made by waving a flag in the daytime and a lantern, or torch, at night. The different waves—right, left, right-left, left-right, right-left-right, and so on—signified different letters of the alphabet, as dots and dashes do in the telegraphic code.

Besides the stations established to keep the various headquarters of the army in communication with one another and connect the commanding General with the nearest telegraph office, there were outlook stations to observe and report the movements of the enemy. Sometimes these were so isolated and exposed that the men occupying them were constantly in danger of being raided and killed or captured. This danger, however, was not without some measure of compensation; for it kept the men on the alert, and prevented the situation from becoming monotonously wearisome. Danger and dullness don't dwell together.

What I regarded as my greatest gain in entering the signal service was having a horse to take the place of "shanks' mare." In my experience as a soldier, that which I found hardest and disliked most was the marching—the toilsome trudging along dusty highways, under a scorching sun, with sore feet and tired limbs and aching muscles, carrying a heavy musket and accouterments that seemed to become heavier every hour, and enduring the nasty, slimy feel of mingled dust and sweat on face and body. And, when the day's march was ended, there was no chance, as a rule, for a cool, cleansing, and refreshing bath. One could only stretch himself on the ground, sleep off as much of his fatigue as possible, and be roused by the reveille next morning to go through another day of weary trudging and add another to the layers of dirt and sweat already accumulated on his body. This to me was the most trying part of a soldier's life. I made no claim to exceptional bravery. It is true that I lost all sense of fear in the excitement of battle, as I think most men do; but I was very much afraid, when going into battle and having time to think of the danger. Yet, there were many times when I would have gladly gone into a fight to stop the wearisome tramp, tramp, tramp of the march. Hence, I highly appreciated the advantage of getting into a branch of the service in which the men were mounted.

I had, however, to provide a mount at my own expense. On reporting for duty, I was told that the first thing for me to do was to buy a horse. Although I was fairly well supplied with Confederate money, buying a good saddle-horse—one that I wouldn't be ashamed to ride—was not as easy as might be supposed. Such horses were scarce in the country, most of them having been taken by the cavalry; and the owners of the few that could be found were not yearning to sell them for Confederate money. But, after looking around for several days, I managed to get a tolerably good mount for $2500.00, the owner protesting that he let the animal go at such a price as a special favor to me.

Having purchased my horse, I returned to the army and entered upon my new service, which I found neither difficult nor unpleasant. The signal code was quickly memorized so that I could send or take messages without the slightest trouble; and the messages, passing to and fro, gave me interesting news, and enabled me to get a clearer insight into conditions and plans than the man in the ranks could have. The man in the signal service often got wind of contemplated moves, and obtained information that it was important to keep secret.

At that time, the two armies were facing each other along the Rapidan—the main body of the Federals being in the vicinity of Culpeper Courthouse, and the Confederates being on the south side of the river, guarding the fords. The signal station to which I was assigned was on Clarke's Mountain—a large hill near the river, from the summit of which, with the aid of a telescope, one could plainly see the camps of the Federals and the movements of the men. On several occasions, General Lee and other officers came up the mountain to make observations, but no important change in the disposition of the Federal forces was seen. For about two months, both armies remained inactive.

One day near the 1st of October, General Lee, with only one attendant as I remember, rode up to our station, dismounted, and, after closely scrutinizing the enemy's position, turned his field-glass westward, and appeared to be carefully examining the lay of the land between the Federal camps and the Blue Ridge. After this examination, he seated himself on a large rock, and remained there for fully half an hour, apparently buried in thought. Then, without a word to any one, he remounted his horse and rode slowly down the mountain. When he was out of hearing, one of the signal men— a shrewd fellow from Louisiana—said: "If I read the signs aright, Marse Robert is studying out some move against the Yankees; and, from the way he kept his field-glass bearing on the country between them and the mountains, I'll bet my pile he's going to make a try at their right flank."

He read the signs aright. About a week later, the army received marching orders, and, crossing the Rapidan at the upper fords, moved to the vicinity of Madison Courthouse. Thence, by a circuitous route, it moved northward along the rough roads through the foothills of the Blue Ridge, with the intention of unexpectedly striking the Federal flank from the direction of the mountains. But the Federal Commander learned of the movement in time to hurriedly withdraw his army to the north side of the Rappahannock.

General Lee then determined on a flanking movement similar to that which had been so successfully carried out against Pope; but General Meade, doubtless having the fate of Pope in mind, was not to be "caught napping." He made haste to escape, and circumstances favored him. The rations with which the man started having been consumed, General Lee was compelled to await the arrival of supplies; and, owing to this delay, when the head of the Confederate column reached Bristoe Station the Federal army, with the exception of a strong rear-guard, had passed that point. This rear-guard, commanded I was told by General Warren, was rashly attacked by the advance brigade of Confederates; but, being skillfully posted behind a railroad embankment, it repulsed the assailants with considerable loss. Thus General Meade not only escaped, but struck a stinging blow in escaping. In this campaign of maneuvering, the advantage was unquestionably with him.

His plan having failed, General Lee, taking time to tear up many miles of the railroad track, withdrew his army to its former position on the south side of the Rapidan; and the Federals, repairing the railroad as they advanced, were soon back in the fields of Culpeper.

The next move in the game was made by General Meade, who, near the end of November, crossed the Rapidan at the lower fords with the intention of making an unexpected attack on the Confederate right. This movement had hardly got well under way before it was reported to General Lee, who, instead of seeking safety in retreat as the Federal Commander had done, changed front and, facing his army eastward along Mine Run, challenged his adversary to battle. But, tempering valor with discretion, General Meade declined the challenge. After two or three days of reconnoitering, he retreated in the night and returned to Culpeper.

His retreat was just in time to avoid a battle; for, finding that the enemy would not attack him, General Lee determined to attack the enemy. Orders were issued and arrangements made to assail the Federal left early on the morning of December 2nd, but, when the morning dawned, the Federals were so far advanced on their way back to their old quarters that pursuit was in vain.

It has been said that General Meade ordered an attack upon the Confederate position, and that it was not made because every soldier in the column selected for the assault silently protested against it, by pinning on his breast a piece of paper with his name written on it to identify his body after the battle. I do not vouch for the truth of this story; but, if true, it shows that the veterans of the Army of the Potomac, whose experience had made them fairly good judges in the matter, regarded the situation pretty much as those of the Army of Northern Virginia did. The Confederates were eager to be attacked. They appreciated the advantage of their position; were confident of their ability to hurl back an assaulting column with frightful loss; and eagerly wished to be assailed, that they might have an opportunity to wipe out the humiliation of their repulse at Gettysburg.

After the Mine Run affair, both armies settled down in their quarters for the winter. I was stationed on the top of Clarke's Mountain, and my old regiment was encamped near its base. I frequently went down to spend a few hours with my friends. The men of the regiment were cheerful and jovial, making the most of what they had and making merry over their privations. This spirit was manifested by the soldiers throughout the army. And, as an evidence of their devotion to the cause in which they were enlisted and their willingness to deny themselves for its sake, let it be remembered that one of the privations about which they jested was the lack of a sufficiency of food—a lack which would have caused the soldiers of almost any other army to mutiny. With much of her most productive territory in the hands of the enemy and with very inadequate facilities for transportation, the South was finding it impossible to properly provision her armies. The soldiers were put on short and still shorter rations. At that time, if I remember rightly, the men of the Army of Northern Virginia were getting only a fourth, and sometimes less than a fourth, of the food usually allowed to soldiers for subsistence. Yet, there was no word of complaint from them. No soldiers ever endured privations and hardships more cheerfully. "In weariness and painfulness, in watchings often, in hunger and thirst, in fastings often, in cold and nakedness," they stood loyally by their colors, murmured not at their discomforts, and made jests about their sufferings.

Some of them, however, undertook to add a little to their scanty supply of food by stealing out of camp, with their guns and cartridges, and shooting a few of the squirrels that could be found everywhere in the woods on the sides of the mountain. For two or three days, there was wafted up to us stationed on the mountain's summit a sound of firing like that of a small skirmish. Of course, such a waste of ammunition could not be tolerated. The offenders were reprimanded and ordered not to repeat the offense. To enforce this order, they were told that their cartridge-boxes would be inspected before each pay-day, and that, for every cartridge missing from any man's box, twenty-five cents would be deducted from his monthly pay. The men obeyed the order.

CHAPTER IX

From the Rapidan to the James

Throughout the winter of 1863–4, all was quiet along our front on the Rapidan. Not even "a stray picket was shot." From the first week in December, when we returned from Mine Run, until the earth was released from the freezing clutch of winter and basking in the genial warmth of May, I did not hear a hostile shot fired by either army.

About the 1st of March, from our station on the mountain we noticed signs of activity in the enemy's camp, and two or three army corps moved up towards Madison Courthouse as if intending to assail the Confederate left; but that proved to be nothing more than a demonstration in force to keep General Lee's attention fixed on his left while General Kilpatrick, with a large body of picked cavalry, was crossing the river below his right, and rapidly pushing on towards Richmond with the purpose of surprising and capturing that city.

Kilpatrick, with his main body, reached the line of works in front of Richmond, but was there repulsed and compelled to retire by a hastily gathered and motley force of engineer troops, clerks, old men, and boys. A column under Colonel Dahlgren, which had been detached to destroy the Central Railroad and the James River Canal, met with a still worse fate. Dahlgren, delayed it is said by a negro guide who didn't like the Yankees and intentionally misled him, failed to effect a junction with the main body before Richmond, was easily put to flight when he arrived there, and, while seeking to make his escape, was killed in an encounter with a company of home guards.

On Dahlgren's body were found papers directing that, in case of the capture of Richmond, "Jeff Davis and Cabinet" were to be killed and the city was to be sacked and burned. The Federal Authorities, and Generals Meade and Kilpatrick also, disclaimed responsibility for these atrocious orders. It has been stated that General Kilpatrick, when shown a photographic copy of them, declared it to be "a facsimile of an address which Dahlgren had submitted to him for approval," but which he did not approve. Who issued them was never ascertained. It is not probable that Dahlgren wrote them for his own guidance, or that he would have accepted them, if they had not come from some official authority that he felt bound to recognize. The facts brought to light seem to indicate that they were issued by some high official in Washington, and were without any evidence of their source in order that the Government might be able to deny responsibility in case of the perpetration of the atrocities enjoined. Of Dahlgren, a distinguished Southern officer said: "His soldierly spirit abhorred the duty that had been assigned him."

While the Federal cavalry was raiding in their rear and creating considerable excitement in Richmond and the counties through which the raiders passed, the infantry along the Rapidan knew nothing of it. Had they known of it, I think it would not have disturbed them; for they thought of cavalry raids, whether Federal or Confederate, as more dashing than dangerous. They were disposed to make game of the cavalry. One day, as an infantry regiment was passing a wounded cavalryman who was being carried to the rear, I heard along the line such jocular remarks as the following:

"Say, boys, there's been an accident; a cavalryman's been wounded."

"Poor fellow! He must be a raw recruit, for he didn't know that the first duty of a cavalryman is to keep out of danger."

"May be the Yanks crept up on him when he was asleep."

"Don't be too hard on the cavalry, boys. It's hard to keep from running away from the Yanks sometimes, when a fellow has only two legs to run on; and when he has four legs, like a cavalryman, he's just bound to skedaddle."

Such remarks called forth by the sight of a wounded man may seem heartless, but they were not. They merely showed the disposition of the soldiers to make light of misfortune as the best way to meet it. They were sorry for the wounded man; but they felt that, even if he heard what they said, he would understand the spirit in which they said it, and would be helped by their laughter far more than he could be by any dolorous expressions of sympathy.

Although the men of the infantry were disposed to banter the cavalry, they appreciated the usefulness of that branch of the service, and did not really doubt that the men who followed Stuart were as courageous as themselves. But they believed that nothing of very great importance—nothing of a decisive character—could be achieved without the help of the infantry—that it was for the infantry to do the really hard fighting and accomplish decisive results.

And, in view of their depleted ranks—seeing so many companies that had entered the war with the complement of one hundred well-conditioned men reduced to two or three dozen ragged and hungry-looking survivors—the more thoughtful among them looked forward to the campaign of the coming summer with a good deal of apprehension. They were still confident of success; but they thought they would have to overcome greater odds than they had yet encountered to win it, and expected to have their courage and endurance severely tested.

The campaign opened in the first week of May. General Grant had been promoted to the command of all the Federal Armies, and had come from the West to personally direct the movements of the Army of the Potomac. That army then numbered over 140,000 well-clothed, well-fed, and thoroughly equipped soldiers, and had a reserve force of almost as many thousands from which to draw reinforcements as they might he needed. To oppose this great army, General Lee had less than 60,000 men, who were deficient in almost all the equipments of war except soldierly qualities. They were men of indomitable courage, determined to make up for the great odds against them by bravely and stubbornly fighting. They were accustomed to fighting against odds; and, although they had not been victorious at Sharpsburg and Gettysburg, they had fought the enemy to a "stand off" in both of those battles. They had never been vanquished.

And General Grant apparently thought they could not be vanquished, except by killing them off regardless of the loss that would be sustained by his own army in so doing. Estimating that, with the present and obtainable force at his command, he could outwear the Confederates even if he sacrificed half a dozen of his own soldiers to kill or cripple one of Lee's, his policy, as stated by himself, was "to hammer continuously against the armed force of the enemy and his resources, until by mere attrition, if by nothing else, there should be nothing left to him" but submission. The adoption of such a policy was a tacit acknowledgment of the superior soldiership of the Army of Northern Virginia and the superior military genius of its commander.

To initiate his "hammering" policy, General Grant crossed the Rapidan about ten miles below the Confederate right, and began his advance on Richmond along the road leading through the Wilderness in which General Hooker had been defeated a year before. Instead of hastening to place his army between the Federals and Richmond, as his opponent evidently expected him to do, General Lee concentrated his forces in the western edge of the Wilderness, and compelled Grant to give battle in that densely wooded region, where his great superiority in numbers would be largely neutralized.

The character of the country in that region, and all along the route followed by the army on its way from the Rapidan to the James, made the establishment of a line of signal stations impracticable, and throughout the campaign the signal corps was of little service to General Lee. General Grant, however, had the best possible means of communication. He says in his Memoirs that, wherever there was a halt, telegraphic wires connecting his corps and division commanders with one another and with himself were laid at once, so that he could instantly direct the movements of every part of his army. This gave him a great advantage; for, in the disposition of troops in a battle, a few minutes may mean victory or defeat.

On the morning of May 5th, our advance brigades came upon a strong force of Federals a mile or two beyond Locust Grove, and the soldiers told a rather amusing story about a well-known chaplain who unexpectedly found himself in the zone of danger. As the story ran, the chaplain, ignorant of the proximity of the enemy and apprehending no danger, was riding along the old turnpike where one could see scarcely ten paces on either side of him when he was startled by the sound of near-by firing and the zip of passing bullets. Whirling his horse, he was making for the rear under whip and spur when he met General Early, who humorously said: "Ah, yes. That's the way of you preachers. You tell us what a good place heaven is; but, when you get a chance to go there, you run away from it." Years afterwards, I told this story in the presence of the chaplain and some of his brethren of the cloth; but, turning red to the roots of his hair, he indignantly denied its truth. Yet he had no reason to be ashamed; for it is truly the part of wisdom to hurriedly leave the zone of danger when one can do no good by staying in it.

The Battle of the Wilderness was fought on the 5th and 6th of May. It was a fierce struggle, in which the contending forces were compelled to grope their way through the thicket to find each other. A northern writer, after describing the thicket that covered the ground on which it was fought as "a dense undergrowth of low-limbed and scraggy pines, stiff and bristling chinkapins, scrub oaks, and hazel," said: "It is a region of gloom and the shadow of death.

The Battle of the Wilderness
(May 5-6, 1864)
Heavy fighting took place in the thickets of the Wilderness.

J. W. Bliley Funeral Homes, Richmond, Va.

Maneuvering there was necessarily out of the question, and only Indian tactics told. The troops could only receive direction by a point of the compass, for not only were the lines of battle entirely hidden from the sight of the commander, but no officer could see ten files on each side of him. Artillery was wholly ruled out of use; the massive concentration of three hundred guns stood silent, and only an occasional piece or section could be brought into play in the roadsides. Cavalry was still more useless. But in that horrid thicket there lurked two hundred thousand men, and through it lurid fires played, and, though no array of battle could be seen, there came out of its depths the roll and crackle of musketry like the noisy boiling of some hell-caldron that told the dread story of death."

After two days of fierce fighting, Grant became convinced that he could not beat Lee in this jungle, and determined to draw him from his position by moving to Spottsylvania Courthouse and threatening to turn his right flank and get between him and Richmond. This he was able to do without danger; for, as Taylor in *Four Years with General Lee* has said: "In numerical strength his army so much exceeded that under General Lee that, after covering the entire Confederate front with double lines of battle, he had in reserve a large force with which to extend his flank and compel a corresponding movement on the part of his adversary, in order to keep between him and his coveted prize—the capital of the Confederacy."

By extending his right to Spottsylvania Courthouse, Grant gained little or nothing; for General Lee, divining his purpose, promptly took measure that defeated it. He dispatched Longstreet's corps by a night-march to Spottsylvania Courthouse; and, when the advance columns of Grant's army, driving the Confederate cavalry before them, reached that point next morning, they found themselves, much to their surprise, faced by a line of infantry that poured into their ranks a musketry fire which drove them back in confusion.

Defeated in his attempt to get around the right flank of the Confederate line, General Grant resorted to his "hammering" tactics, and tried to batter his way through. After spending a day in bringing up his army and strengthening his position, during which time General Lee was doing the same thing, he began a vigorous offensive. Assault after assault was made upon the Confederate line; but, although the Federals advanced with splendid courage and fought most valiantly, the assaulting columns were repulsed with frightful loss.

For a short while, it looked as if one of these attacks might be successful. Before dawn on the 12th of May, when a heavy fog was increasing the obscurity of the night, General Hancock's corps moved up to a salient on General Ewell's front without being observed, and surprised and captured the division that occupied it. Elated with their easily won success, the Federals thronged through this wide breach, confident of carrying everything before them; but their on-rush was checked by a deadly fire from infantry hastily thrown into line across the base of the salient and artillery on the surrounding hills. Though checked, the Federals were not disposed to give up the advantage they had won without a desperate struggle, and the fight developed into one of the fiercest and bloodiest battles of the war. It continued from early morning until late in the afternoon, each side hurrying up reinforcements where they were needed. The Federals, having been constantly repulsed and having lost enormously in killed and wounded, finally withdrew from the contest.

According to the statement of its historian, the bloody repulses suffered by the Army of the Potomac in the fighting around Spottsylvania Courthouse discouraged the men and made them rather eager to get away from that vicinity. He says: "Before the lines of Spottsylvania the Army of the Potomac had . . . engaged in a fierce wrestle in which it had done all that valor may do to carry a position by nature and art impregnable. In this contest, unparalleled in its continuous fury and swelling to the proportions of a campaign, language is inadequate to convey an impression of the labors, fatigues, and sufferings of the troops, who fought by day only to march by night from point to point of the long line, and renew the fight on the morrow. Above 40,000 men had already fallen in the bloody encounters of the Wilderness and Spottsylvania, and the exhausted army began to lose its spirits. It was with joy, therefore, that it at length turned its back upon the lines of Spottsylvania."

After being heavily reinforced to make up for his enormous losses thus far in the campaign, General Grant made another flank march, having as his objective point Hanover Junction, a few miles south of the north Anna River, where the railroad from Fredericksburg to Richmond crosses that from Gordonsville to Richmond. But again he was forestalled. When he reached the vicinity of the Junction on the 23rd, he found the Confederates in position on the south side of the North Anna River to oppose him; and, after two or three days of reconnoitering and some little fighting, he declared "the enemy's position on the North Anna stronger than either of his previous ones," and deemed it advisable to forego his "hammering" process for a time and proceed with his flank march.

Thus Grant moved to his left from point to point and his alert and resourceful adversary anticipated and blocked his every move, until the two armies faced each other at Cold Harbor, where McClellan had been signally defeated nearly two years before. There, on the 3rd of June, General Grant resumed his "hammering" policy, and "massing the flower of his army," vainly attempted to storm the Confederate position. His assailing columns were decimated and hurled back by the Confederate fire. The ground in front of the Confederate works was strewn with Federal dead and wounded; and it is said that the Federal Commander finally desisted from his murderous attempts only because his soldiers refused to again expose themselves to useless slaughter. The corps commanders were directed to renew the assault, but, when the men were ordered to advance, they refused to go forward. With this silent censure of their Commander, the battle ended. The time of actual fighting was about an hour; and the Federals lost 13,000 men in killed and wounded, while the Confederate loss was not much over 1,000.

The battle of Cold Harbor closed the campaign from the Rapidan to the James. Having been foiled in every attempt to break through or get around the Confederate lines, and having lost more men than Lee had in his entire army at the beginning of the campaign, Grant made no further offensive north of the James; and, after about ten days of inactivity, he crossed to the south side of that river.

Swinton puts Grant's loss in this campaign at over 60,000 men, and it is said that "a more careful examination of the figure will show that his real loss was nearer 100,000." If sacrificing that number of men to gain a position which, by the use of railroads and transports, could have been easily and quickly reached without the loss of a man shows great generalship, Grant unquestionably proved himself to be a Great General.

Two or three days after the battle of Cold Harbor, General Lee did the only thing I ever knew him to do which did not have my hearty approval. As all was quiet in our front, another signal man and myself decided to ride down to the Chickahominy bottom, where grass was still to be found, and give our horses a little grazing. Between our camp and the river, the public road made a wide half-circle around the base of a hill that gradually sloped up, for nearly a mile, to a house where General Lee had his headquarters. There was a private road, leading by the house, which cut off this long bend, and we took it. As we neared the house, General Lee, attended by several officers and couriers, rode out and came towards us. We drew to one side to let him pass; but, instead of passing, he stopped and asked where we were going. When we told him, he said: "This is a private way that you have no right to use. Go back to the public road and follow it to your destination." He waved his hand to indicate that we must precede him, and, crestfallen, we started back. The constant going to and from headquarters had pulverized the dry ground, and our horses raised a cloud of dust that enveloped him. Seeing this, my companion, a nervy young thoroughbred, wheeled his horse, saluted, and said: "General, we deserve to be punished, but we beg that you will make our punishment less severe by permitting us to ride in the rear, so that you will not get the dust we raise." Instead of making him a captain and me a lieutenant, as the young fellow afterwards said Napoleon would have done, General Lee, striving in vain to hide a smile, merely thanked us for wishing to save him from discomfort and made us move on. He made us ride before him and throw dust in his face all the way back to that public road. I didn't approve of it at all.

CHAPTER X

My Term of Enlistment Expires

After the crushing defeat of the Federals at Cold Harbor, it was thought by some that General Lee would take the offensive and attack Grant; and probably he would have done so, but for the fact that he was compelled to weaken his army by sending troops to arrest the progress of General Hunter, who was said to be then near Staunton with only a small force under General Breckenridge to oppose his advance. The 2nd corps, to which I was attached and which was then commanded by General Early, was selected for this purpose. Having been engaged in most of the heavy fighting on the way from the Rapidan to the James and having borne the brunt of the battle at Spottsylvania of the memorable 12th of May, when one of its divisions was surprised and captured and the others repulsed the fierce onset of Hancock's corps, it had sustained heavy losses, and then numbered less than 9,000 men present for duty. The men were in high spirits, however; for, like the rest of Lee's army, they felt that, although their courage and endurance had been severely tested, they had everywhere more than held their own against an enemy greatly outnumbering them.

Before daylight on the morning of June 13th, we started for the Valley; and, marching more than twenty miles each day, reached Charlottesville on the 18th. There it was learned that Hunter had left the vicinity of Staunton, crossed the Blue Ridge into Bedford County, and was moving on Lynchburg, which is sixty miles south-west of Charlottesville. He was said to be then within twenty miles of that city, with only a very small force of cavalry to impede his advance; and our chance of getting there ahead of him seemed small. There was a railroad from Charlottesville to Lynchburg, but no trains were at hand to transport the troops, and when, if at all, they could be obtained was doubtful. But by telegraphing for all the trains on both the roads that ran to Charlottesville, General Early managed to get enough cars to carry about half of his troops. On these, Ramseur's division and a part of Gordon's started for Lynchburg early on the morning of the 17th, and the other half of the small army set out on foot to meet the trains, which were to come back for it. I went with General Ramseur. The condition of the road and rolling-stock and the poor management of things greatly delayed us. The train did not average ten miles an hour, and it was past one o'clock in the afternoon when we reached Lynchburg. The troops that the trains returned for did not arrive until late in the afternoon of the next day.

Early's advance force was just in time to prevent Hunter from capturing the city. The troops were quickly marched out two or three miles on the road along which he was advancing; and the two front brigades had hardly got into position when his columns appeared, driving before them the small body of cavalry that had been trying to retard their march. Finding something more than a weak cavalry force in their front, they halted and, after keeping up a brisk artillery fire until about sunset, bivouacked for the night.

During the next day, there was a little skirmishing, some artillery firing, and an easily repulsed attack on one part of our line to feel our strength; but nothing of importance occurred. Late in the afternoon, when the rest of his troops had arrived, General Early made arrangements to attack at dawn next morning, but when the morning dawned no enemy was in our front. Under cover of the night, Hunter had withdrawn his army, which largely exceeded Early's in numerical strength and hurriedly retreated towards the mountains. We set out in hot pursuit of the enemy, Ramseur's division, with which I went, moving in advance along the road by which he was retreating; and a little before sundown his rear-guard was overtaken at Liberty, twenty-five miles from Lynchburg. General Ramseur quickly deployed his leading brigade, and in a few minutes the Federals were driven through the town.

In this little fight, which was nothing more than a brisk skirmish, I was again wounded. Having taken an order from General Ramseur to the extreme right of the attacking brigade, I was riding back along the line to rejoin him when a bullet plunked into my neck just under the hinge of the jawbone. Luckily, my head was thrown back at the moment, pushing the windpipe forward and drawing the jugular vein backward, so that the ball passed between them without cutting either. I was not knocked from my horse, but lost control of him; and, while I clung to the saddle with both hands, he galloped up to a group of horsemen on a hill in the rear. When he reached the group, I found it to be General Early and his staff. Seeing that I was bleeding freely, the General showed a solicitude that I appreciated, and urged me to hasten to Doctor Morrison, who was on the roadside about half a mile back. I started, but fainted from loss of blood and fell from my horse before going fifty yards. When I returned to consciousness, I was lying on the ground, and a soldier was pouring water on my face from his canteen. He was one of a regiment halted by the roadside, and had run forward to catch me when he saw me reeling and about to fall. Without doubt, his kindness and prompt assistance saved me from serious injury. I was taken back to Doctor Morrison on a stretcher, and, after dressing my wound, he had me placed on a cot in a house near the road, where I received every possible attention. The next day, I was taken to a hospital in Liberty, where others who had been wounded in the skirmish were being cared for.

After the first night, during which I suffered excruciating pain, my wound gave little trouble, and I was soon on my feet again. One morning, when I had been in Liberty about ten days, I chanced to meet an old gentleman who was on his way to Lynchburg in a buggy and kindly consented to take me with him.. He was driving a horse that, like himself, had lost the "vim' and 'go" of youth; and, although the road was good, we did not reach Lynchburg until dusk. I went to the home of an acquaintance—a teacher whose pupil I had been when a boy—who welcomed me cordially, gave me an excellent supper, and lodged me for the night. After breakfast next morning, I went to the railway station and boarded a train that took me to Louisa Courthouse in time to hire a conveyance and reach home that evening.

I was wounded on the 19th of June, and returned to the army on the 6th of the following September. In the meantime, General Early, with an army of about ten thousand to start with, having disposed of Hunter by driving him across the Blue Ridge and into the western mountains, had proceeded down the Valley; driven the Federals from Martinsburg and Harper's Ferry; crossed into Maryland and defeated General Lew Wallace at Monocacy; marched to within sight of Washington and frightened the authorities into drawing a large force from Grant's army to defend that city; returned to the lower Valley and routed the forces of Crook and Averill that followed him; and successfully fought a number of minor engagements. He was then north of Winchester, confronting Sheridan and an army more than four times as large as his own, and immeasurably better supplied and equipped. He subsequently met with defeat and disaster, but his achievements up to that time were such as any military commander might be proud of. And for the subsequent disaster he cannot be justly blamed; for he was overwhelmed by numbers and encountered difficulties that no military genius could have overcome. I believe that, under the same conditions, neither "Stonewall" Jackson nor General Lee himself could have averted disaster.

On reporting for duty, I was sent to a station on a spur of Little North Mountain southwest of Winchester—one of a line of stations connecting with the nearest telegraph office, which was then at New Market. It was also in direct communication with a station on the Blue Ridge northeast of Winchester, which overlooked the field of the enemy's operations.

About the middle of September, I received and forwarded along the line to General Early a message from General Lee saying that, according to reports made to him, Grant was being reinforced by troops from the Valley. To this General Early replied: "No troops have left my front." The next day—the afternoon of the 16th, I think it was—General Lee sent another message saying, in substance: "My scouts report a heavy column of infantry and a division of cavalry from your front landed at City Point. Would it not be well to make a reconnaissance in force and ascertain the truth of this?" Although General Early does not say so in his account of the matter, I believe that this message from General Lee was his chief reason for making the expedition to Bunker Hill and Martinsburg with the divisions of Rodes and Gordon, and leaving only Ramseur's division, which numbered less than 2,000 men, in front of Sheridan's main body near Berryville.

At daylight on the morning of September 19th, when the divisions of Gordon and Rodes had got only as far as Stephenson's Depot on their way back from Bunker Hill, Sheridan attacked Ramseur, evidently expecting to easily drive back the small force left in his front and get behind the rest of Early's army. But Ramseur's resolute veterans—in numerical strength less than two full regiments—fought valiantly and stubbornly, and held the enemy in check from dawn until ten o'clock, when the other divisions arrived. These, quickly formed into line and ordered forward, assailed the enemy's attacking columns with courage and determination, threw them into confusion, and drove them from the field. "This attacking force of the enemy," says General Early, "proved to be the 6th and 19th corps, and it was a grand sight to see this immense body hurled back in utter disorder before my two divisions, numbering a very little over 5,000 muskets."

A little later, the outlook station on the Blue Ridge signaled: "Hurrah! We've whipped them. Their wagon-trains are scurrying to the rear, their ranks are in great confusion, and they are making preparations for retreat." But one of their so-called preparations for retreat turned the tide of battle in their favor and proved disastrous to us. To draw attention from his front and enable his defeated corps to safely retire, as the observers on the Blue Ridge thought, Sheridan sent a large force of cavalry, supported by infantry that had not been engaged, along the Martinsburg road to the left of the Confederate line, when General Early, with the troops at his disposal, had been able to place only a small and inadequate guard. This overwhelming force—two divisions of cavalry and a corps of infantry—easily drove back the small body of troops that opposed them, and some of the cavalry dashed on towards Winchester. Before it reached the town, however, it was met and repulsed by two or three brigades of infantry that had double-quicked to intercept it.

But the fight in their rear caused confusion among the men in front, who, hearing the firing behind them and supposing that the Federals had got in their rear and were about to cut them off, began to fall back. Seeing this, the Federals advanced boldly; but their progress was retarded by a small force posted behind old breast-works just north of Winchester, until a new line could be formed south of the town. This new line held the enemy in check until night, and General Early then retired to Newtown.

General Early's defeat at Winchester was due neither to bad generalship on his part nor to lack of valor on the part of his soldiers, but to the immense numerical superiority of his adversary. Sheridan's cavalry alone was fully equal in numerical strength to Early's whole army; his artillery, in both guns and men, greatly exceeded that of the Confederates; and his infantry, as a careful examination of the figures given by Federal officials will show, numbered not less than 30,000. Yet, had there been a single division of fresh troops at his command to follow up the success won about noon, or had there been a barely sufficient force at his disposal to protect his left afterwards, I believe General Early would have won a complete and brilliant victory that day, and the fame of "Old Jube" might have rivaled that of "Stonewall" Jackson.

The next morning the army, unmolested by the enemy, moved back to Fisher's Hill, just south of Strasburg, and took up a position between the Massanutten and the Little North Mountains. With two other signal men, I was sent to the top of the Massanutten Mountain, which overlooks the country towards Winchester, to observe and report the movements of the enemy. As signal men stationed there had been attacked and driven away on a previous occasion, a small guard was sent along for our protection.

That afternoon Sheridan's advance forces reached Cedar Creek, not four or five miles from Early's position; and the next day the turnpike between Winchester and Strasburg was blue with long lines of infantry and artillery coming up. The Federals gradually pushed forward, forcing back our skirmishers; and, on the morning of the 22nd, occupied a strong position almost within musketshot of the Confederate front. About the middle of the afternoon, we saw a heavy column of infantry moving into the woods along the foot of Little North Mountain, with the obvious intention of turning the left flank of the Confederates. This movement was, of course, immediately reported to General Early; but, as the message was being signaled to him, it was evident to us, looking down on the two armies in the valley below, that he had no means of providing against an attack from that quarter. His line was so attenuated that he could not move troops from any point to protect his left without leaving a gap through which the Federals, who were massed along his entire front, could rush without opposition. One of the men with me said: "It's rumored that 'Old Jube' isn't given to praying, as they say 'Stonewall' Jackson was; but, if he ever does pray, I think he must now be imploring the Lord to hurry up the coming of night. If night doesn't come before the Yankees swarm down upon him from the mountain and hurl their masses against his front, nothing short of a miracle can save him." The Yankees swarmed upon his flank and front just before sunset, and no miracle was wrought to avert disaster. After bravely resisting until they saw that resistance was useless, the Confederates retreated up the Valley.

Left on the mountain, in rear of the pursuing Federals, we debated as to how we could get out of our predicament. The officer in command of the fifteen or twenty men who had been sent up to guard the station decided to take them south along the top of the mountain until he got ahead of the advance pursuers, and then descend into the Valley to rejoin his regiment. Whether or not he succeeded in this attempt to get back to his command, I never learned. My two companions and myself decided upon what we thought an easier and quicker, though more circuitous, route. Feeling our way in the darkness, we stumbled down into Powell's Fort Valley, between the two branches of the Massanutten at its northern end, and there found comfortable quarters for the night. The next day, we climbed over the east branch of the Massanutten, made our way across the Luray Valley, where we were fired upon by a party of Federal cavalry and barely escaped capture; and reached a resting place in a gap of the Blue Ridge about night, thoroughly exhausted by our march. From that point we went to Culpeper Courthouse, and thence by railroad to the upper Valley, where we rejoined our army.

About a week later the enemy, frightened I suppose by reports of reinforcements coming to us from Richmond, began to retire down the Valley. General Early quickly followed; but being assigned to a relay station, I did not go with the army, and was not in close touch with the operations that led up to the Battle of Cedar Creek and the events that immediately followed it.

When our army was moved back to the upper Valley, sometime after the battle of Cedar Creek, I was sent to a station at Thornton's Gap in the Blue Ridge, which, in connection with lookout stations at Ashby's Gap and on the Massanutten Mountain, kept General Early informed of what Sheridan was doing. He refers to this line of stations in his "Last Year of the War," in which he says: "The telegraph to New Market and the signal stations from there to the lower Valley were kept up, . . . and in this way was my front principally picketed, and I kept advised of the enemy's movements."

I remained at Thornton's Gap until the last of February, 1865, when Sheridan's rapid advance up the Valley rendered the station useless and I was ordered to report at headquarters. After a long and wearisome ride, I reached Waynesboro on the morning of March 2nd, and there found General Early with the nearest regiment of an army. Kershaw's division and the whole of the 2nd corps had been sent to General Lee; the cavalry and most of the artillery had been sent where forage could be found for the horses; and two so-called brigades, numbering not more than one full regiment, with a few pieces of artillery constituted his entire force.

It was a cheerless morning. Leaden clouds hung over the country and a freezing drizzle was falling. In the afternoon, a column of Sheridan's cavalry swooped down on the wet and shivering little force and, sweeping around its flank and getting between it and the mountain, captured nearly all of it.

I made my escape by running into the woods on the south side of the road leading through Rockfish Gap. I had barely crossed the road and dropped exhausted in the thick undergrowth beyond it, when a company of Yankee cavalry rode past me at a furious pace, bound, as I supposed, for Rockfish Gap and the eastern side of the Blue Ridge Mountains.

Having rested awhile after my exhausting run for cover, I started up the mountain, with the intention of getting to the eastern side that night; but a dense fog, making it impossible for me to keep my bearings, soon arrested my progress. I spent that night on the western slope of the mountain, in snow not less than a foot deep, and without overcoat, blanket, or fire. By stirring around and vigorously exercising, I managed to keep from freezing.

Next morning I made my way to the east side of the Blue Ridge, and entered the beautiful Piedmont Valley. Small detachments of Federal cavalry were raiding through the country in every direction. About noon, having had nothing to eat for more than twenty-four hours, I was quite hungry; and, after carefully reconnoitering, left the brush and went to a house near the foot of the mountain to ask for food. The proprietor, an old man, received me hospitably, gave me a dinner "fit for a king," supplied me with food enough for a week's journey, and, as I was leaving, presented me with a quart of peach brandy made by himself, fourteen years old, and the best I ever tasted. Keeping close watch on the movements of the raiding parties and moving with caution, I succeeded in getting clear of the enemy's reach that night.

After the Waynesboro affair, there was no Confederate army in the Valley; but an outpost of twenty or thirty horsemen was stationed at New Market, and I was sent to that place. I had been there not more than a week, when the line of communication was broken and we could get no news from the eastern side of the Blue Ridge. A few days later, a ragged, dust-covered, and tired-looking man, mounted on a lean and tired-looking horse, rode into the little town and told us that General Lee had surrendered. One of the men near me whipped out his pistol and said: "You're a d——d deserter and liar; and, if you say again that General Lee has surrendered, I'll shoot you." The tired horseman looked at him coolly for a moment, and then, pulling open his torn and stained gray shirt and exposing his naked breast, said: "Well, I don't see much worth living for now, and I'd about as soon die as not; for what I've told you is God's truth. General Lee has surrendered. Shoot."

Unexpected and grievous as the news was, his tone and bearing convinced us of its truth. We begged his pardon for having doubted him at first, and asked him to give us the particulars of the surrender. Now and then choking down a sob, he told the sad story of Appomattox. Grant's policy of defeating Lee "by mere attrition" had finally succeeded. The Army of Northern Virginia, which, notwithstanding his vastly greater numerical strength, had everywhere defeated him in the campaign of 1864, had at last been worn down by his "hammering" to a mere handful of men as compared with their foes; and these, half starved, subsisting on meager supplies of parched corn, and hemmed in by a great host of assailants, but still unvanquished in spirit, had lowered their battle-torn banners and laid down their arms, not because they were unwilling to fight on to the death, but in obedience to the command of their wise and great-hearted leader, who would not permit them to sacrifice themselves in an utterly hopeless struggle.

Immediately after hearing of Lee's surrender, the little company at New Market met in consultation to decide upon their own course. Every man of them was in favor of riding south to join General Johnston. In less than an hour, we were on our way. When we reached Staunton, we learned that Johnston had surrendered, and our last hope died. The end had come, and with a heavy heart I turned my horse's head eastward and rode home. But I carried with me the consciousness of duty done. I had fulfilled my promise to my dying father that I would serve Virginia as long as she might need my service. I had enlisted for the war; the war was over; the term of my enlistment had expired.

EPILOGUE

Following the war, Rev. Robert Catlett Cave, along with two of his brothers, who had also suffered severe battle wounds, entered the ministry of the Christian Church. He served as a minister in Virginia, Tennessee, Kentucky and Missouri and was President of South Kentucky Female College, Hopkinsville, Kentucky from 1876 to 1880.

In 1892 he toured Europe and Palestine, sponsored by the St. Louis, Missouri, *Republic* Newspaper as the most popular minister in that city. On May 30, 1894, he delivered the oration at the unveiling of the monument to the Confederate Sailors and Soldiers of the Southern Confederacy in Libby Park, Richmond, Virginia. In 1897 he was elected President of Transylvania College in Lexington, Kentucky.

In 1911 he published *The Men in Gray*, and several religious books in 1917–1919. The noted theologian and orator passed away in St. Louis in 1923 at the age of eighty, having had a full, successful, eventful and exemplary life experience.

In 1889 Rev. Cave preached the funeral for the state of Tennessee of President Jefferson Davis before one of the largest congregations ever assembled in the history of the state. The services were held in the state capitol in Nashville.

Confederate Sailors and Soldiers' Monument, Libby Prison Park, Richmond, Virginia

Robert C. Cave

Robert Catlett Cave

1843 Born 13 Feb. Orange Co., Va. son of Robert Cave & Sarah Frances Lindsay Cave.

1859 Entered Bethany College as a new student.

1860 Returned 2nd year.

1860–61 Left school to join Confederate army.

1861–65 Service in Confederate army Co. A, 13th Va. Inf. "Promised dying father to serve Va. as long as she might need his service."

1863 Married Fannie Daniel of Orange Co.

1865–72 No information. He was ordained to ministry of Christian Church and served churches in Orange Co. Macedonia Church Edinburg.

1872 Became Editor of *Apostolic Times* Newspaper of Christian Church in Ky. Edited in Lexington.

1875 Resigned? This was about the time that he later said he became a religious liberal.

1876–80 President of South Kentucky Female College. Hopkinsville, Ky.

1880–83 Minister of Church Street Christian Church in Nashville, Tenn.

1883 Became pastor of 7th St. Christian Church, Richmond, Va.

1885 Resigned.

1886 Returned to Seventh St. Church.

1888 Resigned & moved to St. Louis, Mo.

1888–89 Minister of Central Christian Church St. Louis.

1890 Became pastor of New Congregation formed from Central Christian Church known initially as West End Christian Church ** by 1891 as the Non-Sectarian Church.

1891 Declined Baccalaureate Sermon at University of Missouri.

1892 Toured Europe and Palestine April through August, having won a contest sponsored by St. Louis Republic as the city's most popular minister.

1900 Retired from Pastor of Non-Sectarian Church because of ill health.

1911 Published *The Men in Gray*.

1917 Joined Union Ave. Christian Church.

1917–18 Published *The Immaiul God*.

1918–19 Published *A Manual for Ministers* & *A Manual for Home Devotions*.

1923 Died at his home, 4511 McPherson, St. Louis, Mo.

BIBLIOGRAPHY

Dowdey, Clifford. Lee, Little, Brown & Co., Boston, Mass. 1965.
Historical Times, Ill., Encyclopedia of the Civil War. Patricia Faust, Ed., Harper & Roe, N.Y. 1986.
Price, William H. *Civil War Handbook.* Prince Lithograph Co., Fairfax, Va. 1961.
The Nashville Tennesseean. Nashville, Tenn. July 8, 1923.

INDEX

86